Modes and Meaning: Displays of Evidence in Education

In the past few decades there has been a growing interest and debate amongst historians of education surrounding issues of visuality, materiality, spatiality, transfer, and circulation. This collection of essays – with its focus on the interaction between ideas, images, objects, and/or spaces that contain an educational dimension – is a contribution to this ongoing debate. The contributors address how meaning is created, conveyed, and transformed through multiple modes of communication, representation, and interaction; through movement across spaces; through media and technologies; and through collective memory- and identity-making. The collection demonstrates that meaning is mobilized through 'multimodality', 'translocation', 'technology', and 'heritage', and that it assumes different qualities which need to be reflected upon in the history of education in particular and in education research in general.

This book was originally published as a special issue of *Paedagogica Historica.*

Geert Thyssen is a Senior Lecturer at Liverpool John Moores University, UK, a Research Associate at the University of Liège, Belgium, and a Visiting Scholar at the University of Sassari, Italy. He is also a convenor of the European Educational Research Association's 'Network 17: Histories of Education'. His interests are in education and early childhood studies, and in the social and cultural history of education, with a focus on health, the body, nutrition, and educational reform initiatives, as well as the visual, audio-visual, material, spatial, sensual, and emotional.

Karin Priem is Professor of the History of Education at the University of Luxembourg. She has been president of the German History of Education Association (2007–2011), is a member of the advisory board of the *Revue Suisse des Sciences de l'Education*, is co-editor of two book series, and is currently Executive Secretary of the International Standing Conference for History of Education. Her research focuses on the history of educational theories and concepts, the social, visual, and material history of education, and the history of curriculum and cultural practices.

Modes and Meaning: Displays of Evidence in Education

Edited by
Geert Thyssen and Karin Priem

LONDON AND NEW YORK

First published 2017
by Routledge
2 Park Square, Milton Park, Abingdon, Oxon, OX14 4RN, UK

and by Routledge
711 Third Avenue, New York, NY 10017, USA

Routledge is an imprint of the Taylor & Francis Group, an informa business

© 2017 Stichting Paedagogica Historica

All rights reserved. No part of this book may be reprinted or reproduced or utilised in any form or by any electronic, mechanical, or other means, now known or hereafter invented, including photocopying and recording, or in any information storage or retrieval system, without permission in writing from the publishers.

Trademark notice: Product or corporate names may be trademarks or registered trademarks, and are used only for identification and explanation without intent to infringe.

British Library Cataloguing in Publication Data
A catalogue record for this book is available from the British Library

ISBN 13: 978-1-138-67010-5

Typeset in Times New Roman
by RefineCatch Limited, Bungay, Suffolk

Publisher's Note
The publisher accepts responsibility for any inconsistencies that may have arisen during the conversion of this book from journal articles to book chapters, namely the possible inclusion of journal terminology.

Disclaimer
Every effort has been made to contact copyright holders for their permission to reprint material in this book. The publishers would be grateful to hear from any copyright holder who is not here acknowledged and will undertake to rectify any errors or omissions in future editions of this book.

Contents

Citation Information   vii
Notes on Contributors   ix
Acknowledgements   xi

1. Mobilising meaning: multimodality, translocation, technology and heritage   1
   Geert Thyssen and Karin Priem

2. A poetic journey: the transfer and transformation of German strategies for moral education in late eighteenth-century Dutch poetry for children   11
   Sanne Parlevliet and Jeroen J.H. Dekker

3. Moving frontiers of empire: production, travel and transformation through technologies of display   35
   Natasha Macnab, Ian Grosvenor and Kevin Myers

4. Activism, agency and archive: British activists and the representation of educational colonies in Spain during and after the Spanish Civil War   61
   Siân Roberts

5. The Decorated School: cross-disciplinary research in the history of art as integral to the design of educational environments   78
   Catherine Burke

6. Puppets on a string in a theatre of display? Interactions of image, text, material, space and motion in *The Family of Man* (ca. 1950s–1960s)   93
   Karin Priem and Geert Thyssen

Index   111

Citation Information

The chapters in this book were originally published in *Paedagogica Historica*, volume 49, issue 6 (December 2013). When citing this material, please use the original page numbering for each article, as follows:

Chapter 1
Mobilising meaning: multimodality, translocation, technology and heritage
Geert Thyssen and Karin Priem
Paedagogica Historica, volume 49, issue 6 (December 2013) pp. 735–744

Chapter 2
A poetic journey: the transfer and transformation of German strategies for moral education in late eighteenth-century Dutch poetry for children
Sanne Parlevliet and Jeroen J.H. Dekker
Paedagogica Historica, volume 49, issue 6 (December 2013) pp. 745–768

Chapter 3
Moving frontiers of empire: production, travel and transformation through technologies of display
Natasha Macnab, Ian Grosvenor and Kevin Myers
Paedagogica Historica, volume 49, issue 6 (December 2013) pp. 769–795

Chapter 4
Activism, agency and archive: British activists and the representation of educational colonies in Spain during and after the Spanish Civil War
Siân Roberts
Paedagogica Historica, volume 49, issue 6 (December 2013) pp. 796–812

Chapter 5
The Decorated School: cross-disciplinary research in the history of art as integral to the design of educational environments
Catherine Burke
Paedagogica Historica, volume 49, issue 6 (December 2013) pp. 813–827

CITATION INFORMATION

Chapter 6
Puppets on a string in a theatre of display? Interactions of image, text, material, space and motion in The Family of Man *(ca. 1950s–1960s)*
Karin Priem and Geert Thyssen
Paedagogica Historica, volume 49, issue 6 (December 2013) pp. 828–845

For any permission-related enquiries please visit:
http://www.tandfonline.com/page/help/permissions

Notes on Contributors

Catherine Burke is a Reader in the History of Education and Childhood at the University of Cambridge, UK. Her current research examines the relationship between innovation in teaching and the design of formal and informal learning spaces, the view of the child and young person in the design of education, and the history of twentieth century school architecture and its pioneers. Her most recent book is *The School I'd Like Revisited* (with Ian Grosvenor, 2015).

Jeroen J.H. Dekker is Professor of History and Theory of Education, and Head of the Department of Education, at the University of Groningen, The Netherlands. He is a former president of the International Association for the History of Education, and co-Editor-in-Chief of *Paedagogica Historica*. His publications deal with the social and cultural history of education, childhood, and parenting.

Ian Grosvenor is Professor of Urban Educational History at the University of Birmingham, UK. He is the author of numerous articles and books on racism, education and identity, the visual in educational research, the material culture of education, and the history of urban education. His most recent book is *The School I'd Like Revisited* (with Catherine Burke, 2015).

Natasha Macnab is a Research Fellow in the School of Education at the University of Birmingham, UK. Her work has appeared in *Paedagogica Historica*, the *British Journal of Special Education*, the *European Educational Research Journal*, *Professional Development in Education*, and the *International Journal of Research and Method in Education*.

Kevin Myers is Senior Lecturer in Social History and Education, and Deputy Head of the Department of Education at the University of Birmingham, UK. His research interests include the history of education, and the history and sociology of childhood. His latest book is entitled *Struggles for a Past: Irish and Afro-Caribbean Histories in England, 1951–2000* (2015).

Sanne Parlevliet is a Researcher in the Faculty of Behavioural and Social Sciences at the University of Groningen, The Netherlands. Her work has been published in *History of Education*, *Paedagogica Historica*, the *Journal of Family History*, *Children's Literature in Education*, and *New Voices in Translation Studies*. She is also a children's writer and translator.

Karin Priem is Professor of the History of Education at the University of Luxembourg. She has been president of the German History of Education Association (2007–2011),

NOTES ON CONTRIBUTORS

is a member of the advisory board of the *Revue Suisse des Sciences de l'Education*, is co-editor of two book series, and is currently Executive Secretary of the International Standing Conference for History of Education. Her research focuses on the history of educational theories and concepts, the social, visual, and material history of education, and the history of curriculum and cultural practices.

Siân Roberts is a Researcher in the School of Education at the University of Birmingham, UK. She is also a member of the Birmingham Civic Society's Heritage Committee and the Executive Committee of the History of Education Society UK. Her research focuses on Quaker women educators and their involvement in twentieth century refugee relief and humanitarian activism, and twentieth century educational interventions with children and young people in contexts of war or displacement.

Geert Thyssen is a Senior Lecturer at Liverpool John Moores University, UK, a Research Associate at the University of Liège, Belgium, and a Visiting Scholar at the University of Sassari, Italy. He is also a convenor of the European Educational Research Association's 'Network 17: Histories of Education'. His interests are in education and early childhood studies, and in the social and cultural history of education, with a focus on health, the body, nutrition, and educational reform initiatives, as well as the visual, audio-visual, material, spatial, sensual, and emotional.

Acknowledgements

The editors would like to thank Ian Grosvenor for having made it possible for this book and the special issue upon which it is based to be published. They would also like to thank Marc Depaepe, who acted as Managing Editor for this special issue and supported both volumes through his comments as a discussant at ISCHE Geneva. They would further like to thank the Stichting Paedagogica Historica, the editorial board of *Paedagogica Historica*, and last but not least Nick Barclay, the Routledge Special Issues as Books Editor, for their support. Finally, they would like to thank the University of Luxembourg for financial support, Edward Haasl for his editorial revisions of the introduction, and all those who have contributed to the book and/or special issue through their papers, and/or by sharing ideas and discussions.

Mobilising meaning: multimodality, translocation, technology and heritage

Geert Thyssen and Karin Priem

Languages, Media, Culture and Identity, University of Luxembourg

Introduction

This special issue explores how meaning is created, conveyed and transformed through multiple modes of communication, representation and interaction (the textual, the visual, the material, the spatial, the aural, the imaginary, etc.); through movement across spaces; through media and technologies; and, finally, through collective memory- and identity-making. In short, this issue is concerned with meaning mobilised through "multimodality", "translocation", "technology" and "heritage". As such, it closely connects to several core dimensions of education which in the past few decades have undergone a revival of interest in histories of education: visuality, materiality, spatiality, transfer and circulation. Related to these key education dimensions are issues to do with the diffusion of knowledge, values, practices and ways of seeing, perceiving and feeling across and beyond borders. Such issues were at the heart of a symposium organised at the 34th International Standing Conference for the History of Education (ISCHE), which took place in Geneva in June 2012 in cooperation with the Society for the History of Children and Youth (SHCY) and the Disability History Association (DHA) and addressed the theme of "internationalization in education".[1]

The specific topics addressed in this issue include: (1) the promotion, circulation and reception of educational undertakings through annual reports with photographic material distributed by an internationally active charitable institution and through a reading group campaigning for textbook revisions by means of pamphlets and exhibitions (Macnab, Grosvenor and Myers); (2) the changes of meaning undergone through textual and visual representations of displaced children in educational colonies travelling from Republican Spain to Britain and from networks of humanitarian–pedagogical activism to the archives (Roberts); (3) imaginings of artists, educators and policy-makers materialised in school decoration and the latter's relation to school buildings as well as the education of taste and consumption (Burke); the journey from Germany to the Netherlands of poetry written for children as part of the educational programme of the Enlightenment, its remodelling in the function of new perceptions of the child and of forms of citizenship and its reception and use as illustrated textbooks (Parlevliet and Dekker); and, finally, the educational power

---

[1]See http://www.unige.ch/ische34-shcy-dha/theme_en.html (accessed 28 August 2013).

of interacting images, material objects, spaces and emotions in different cultural settings as exemplified by the travelling photographic exhibition called *The Family of Man* (Priem and Thyssen).

All of the contributions, as diverse as they might seem at first sight, touch on common aspects of meaning-making, all of which relate to transfer and translation and to their materiality or physicality. These common aspects of mobilisation of meaning will be discussed with reference to multimodality, translocation, technology and heritage.

Multimodality

Meaning-making and the modes employed to bring it about refer to cultural practices such as seeing, reading and writing, which in turn involve the handling of things and artefacts. In a discipline like the history of books, this focus on materiality has implied a move away from seeing text as a purely linguistic matter to understanding it as something embedded in a physical–material carrier of which both the structure and the organisation affect the meanings readers bestow on it.[2] Similarly, in visual studies and the history of science, it has been emphasised that images need to be analysed as three-dimensional objects since their physical body and sensorial quality differ in function of the techniques of image-making, the size and format, the levels of abstraction, colour schemes and so on, all of which affect the meanings spectators ascribe to them.[3] From such diverse disciplinary perspectives, different ways of conveyance, perception, practice and handling become issues that are intrinsically bound up with what has been termed "multimodality". Indeed, in all the spheres of social and cultural practice, a multiplicity of communication, representation and interaction modes converge to generate meaning. In promoting educational visions, pursuing educational effects and objectifying results of educational programmes, among other things, the role and dynamics of interacting modes of meaning-making (including such modes as the textual, the visual, the material, the spatial, the sensorial and the bodily) are crucial. For example, from the ways in which texts, words, images, spaces, and so on are mobilised in education as catalysts of meaning, intended and unintended learning effects result, as that which is mediated and perceived in specific temporal-spatial contexts, through these very processes, becomes transformed.

The multimodality of teaching, upbringing and learning, and its far-reaching implications, have yet to be given sufficient attention in the history of education. The research on this subject in the past two decades or so under the umbrella of multimodal studies is still largely confined to the realm of language didactics and

---

[2] Roger Chartier and Guglielmo Cavallo, *A History of Reading in the West* (London: Polity Press, 1999). See also Lynn Fendler and Karin Priem, "Material Contexts and Creation of Meaning in Virtual Places: Web 2.0 as a Space of Educational Research," in *Educational Research. The Importance and Effects of Institutional Spaces*, eds. P. Smeyers, M. Depaepe and E. Keiner (Dordrecht: Springer, 2013), 177–91.
[3] Lorraine J. Daston and Peter L. Galison, *Objectivity* (New York: Zone Books 2007); Swetlana Alpers, *The Art of Describing: Dutch Art in the Seventeenth Century* (Chicago: University of Chicago Press, 1983); Jacques Rancière, *Dissensus: On Politics and Aesthetics* (London: Continuum, 2011); Raymond Williams, *The Long Revolution* (New York: Columbia University Press, 1961).

linguistics or social semiotics.[4] To date, little of the work conducted in these disciplines has found its way into the history of education, some exceptions notwithstanding.[5] Even though multimodality research is a fairly recent and still developing field of study,[6] it has relevance for educational studies in general and for histories of education in particular,[7] especially in view of its awareness that modes of meaning-making are "shaped through their cultural, historical and social uses".[8] The heightened interest in multimodality across disciplines is at least partly due to increasing dissatisfaction with analyses that reduce communication and other forms of meaning-making to the domain of language and discourse. Indeed, multimodality as a concept in itself "understands communication and representation to be more than about language".[9] It instead comprises a "full repertoire of meaning-making resources" used to represent and to create meaning within a set of social and spatial conditions that, in turn (on the side of receivers, consumers or learners), encounter individual selection and "configurations of modes" according to motivation, interest and emotions.[10]

While multimodality is not always explicitly addressed in the contributions to this special issue, it manifests itself as an unspoken concern. Macnab, Grosvenor, and Myers, for instance, analyse how communities of interpretation are formed around interacting texts, images, objects and spaces across borders in two contexts: in the framework of a Birmingham-based charitable institution (The Children's Emigration Homes) that sent poor children to receiving homes and families in Canada and Australia, and in the framework of a public education and campaigning body (the Liverpool Community Relations Council) devoted to "educating away 'prejudice'" against the black community of Liverpool while counteracting "a powerful national master narrative" that silenced key aspects of the city's migration history. Their article touches on different material conditions or "materialities" of texts and images gathered in reports, books (particularly textbooks), pamphlets and an exhibition, each bearing the imprint of their social contexts of production. Thus,

---

[4]For a brief overview of parallel developments in language didactics and linguistics, see, for instance, Ingrid de Saint-Georges, "La multimodalité et ses ressources pour l'enseignement-apprentissage", in *"Vos mains sont intelligentes!": interactions en formation professionnelle initiale*. eds. L. Filliettaz, I. de Saint-Georges and B. Duc (Université de Genève: Cahiers de la section des sciences de l'éducation, 2008), 117–58.

[5]See, for instance, Carey Jewitt and Ken Jones, "Managing Time and Space in the New English Classroom," in *Materialities of Schooling: Design, Technology, Objects, Routines*, eds. M. Lawn and I. Grosvenor (Oxford: Symposium, 2005), 201–14.

[6]The consolidation of this research field is demonstrated by Carey Jewitt, ed., *The Routledge Handbook of Multimodal Analysis* (London & New York: Routledge, 2009). Other work surveying this emerging field of inquiry includes *Multimodal Studies: Exploring Issues and Domains*, eds. K. L. O'Halloran and B. A. Smith (London: Routledge, 2011), 1–3; Gunther Kress, *Multimodality: A Social Semiotic Approach to Contemporary Communication* (London: Routledge, 2010).

[7]A recent example demonstrating this is Ingrid de Saint-Georges and Jean-Jacques Weber, eds., *Multilingualism and Multimodality: Current Challenges for Educational Studies* (Series: The Future of Educational Research, vol. 2) (Rotterdam: Sense, 2012).

[8]Jewitt, ed., *Routledge Handbook of Multimodal Analysis*, 15.

[9]Carey Jewitt, "Multimodality and Digital Technologies in the Classroom," in *Multilingualism and Multimodality*, eds. I. de Saint-Georges and J.-J. Weber, 141. See also, for instance, Carys Jones and Eija Ventola, eds., *From Language to Multimodality. New Developments in the Study of Ideational Meaning* (London: Equinox, 2008).

[10]Jewitt, "Multimodality and Digital Technologies," 142.

for example, within reports of various lengths (and, therefore, of different material make-up), texts – and "statistics" – were juxtaposed in particular ways with before-and-after photographs. The images are generally of poor quality but, in the case of the "after" photographs produced by a more refined form of bourgeois studio photography cleverly using material props, they supported the rhetoric of transformation or progress. Different modes of display thus produced what counted as evidence. Interestingly, texts, numbers or images alone never sufficed to determine constituted "facts". Indeed, the preferred assembly of modes of representation reveals implicit assumptions about the power of combined modes of meaning-making and the inability of a single media form to convey "truth".[11]

Parlevliet and Dekker, while focussing on children's poems by Hieronijmus van Alphen and the illustrations by Jacob Buijs that soon accompanied them, similarly find that precisely the combination of texts and images within certain material carriers was thought to better convey the pedagogical intentions behind the poems. Bundled images and texts were vehicles employed to display closeness to children's family environments and their modes of perception. The putting to music of the children's poems in turn facilitated their interiorisation. Likewise, the spaces in which Van Alphen's poems were consumed – initially mainly the family home, but later on, gradually, above all the school – added different meanings to the poems. Roberts also alludes to the importance and power of spaces – both literal and "performative" ones – where she investigates documentary photographs (as well as postcards and lantern slides) in the context of humanitarian aid and political activism in which various organisations and actors in Birmingham, Spain and other countries were involved. The images and texts she analyses became part not only of overlapping spheres of propaganda, documentation and memory-making, but also of different material constellations, which include archival files, photo binders, reports and pamphlets, each of which afford different possible meanings. Burke shifts attention to architecture, design and decoration. In her contribution, she describes murals and other permanent features of decoration (statues, pillars, etc.) as part of the school fabric in the UK and other countries. As extra-curricular school elements, they were supposed to connect with the world of play of children (in ways similar to Van Alphen's consideration of children's senses as readers/viewers) and, at the same time, to cultivate the taste of these primary "spectators as future consumers". Elements of "The Decorated School", particularly murals, were sometimes purposely integrated in school buildings, and may have produced powerful effects because of their interaction with them as material in terms of size and colour schemes. Finally, Priem and Thyssen explore a travelling photographic exhibition, *The Family of Man*, as a carefully designed multimodal "theatre of display" that combined exhibition-design elements, texts, lighting, spaces, buildings, pace, etc. in an attempt to convey a homogenised, universal view of mankind. The contribution of the intended spectators as consumers and learners is explicitly considered. Their agency is highlighted, as is that of the exhibition-design objects, with reference to the symmetrical anthropology developed by Bruno Latour.[12] In relation to this, it is stressed that

---

[11] Cf. Geert Thyssen, "Visualizing Discipline of the Body in a German Open-Air School (1923–1939): Retrospection and Introspection," *History of Education* 36, no. 2 (2007), 243–60.
[12] Bruno Latour, *Reassembling the Social: An Introduction to Actor-Network Theory* (Oxford: Oxford University Press, 2005).

meaning-making is always subject to uncertain conditions that can be understood also from a multimodal perspective: indeed, learners/spectators/viewers apply different and unexpected modes of meaning-making.

Technology

The modes of meaning-making referred to, of course, depend on technologies and media – which, as Macnab, Grosvenor, and Myers suggest, still largely constitute under-researched subjects in the history of education.[13] Writing, drawing, painting, print and photography, among other technologies, take shape materially in media like books, computer files and images. Involving certain epistemic features that organise reading, viewing, listening, and other techniques or practices (employed individually or in public spaces), such media in themselves "contaminate" what they convey.[14] Media, technologies and cultural techniques alike have been studied in ethnography and anthropology as key elements of human culture and have sometimes been associated with the evolution of the human body, the development of skills and intellectual capacity.[15] Norbert Elias, in his history of the civilisation process[16] and elsewhere, has analysed the transformation of table manners and speech forms as a history of increasing self-control, which needed refined tools and technologies. Technologies are also a central issue in Friedrich Kittsteiner's *Aufschreibesysteme*,[17] a media history that has associated the invention of new technologies with the notion of a growing web of tools and techniques collecting and inscribing data onto material carriers. In addition, with Peter Burke,[18] one could add that one medium reinforces the other, together with the cultural techniques and practices accompanying them. Finally, Roger Chartier and Guglielmo Cavallo, in their history of books, have outlined how different forms of textual media, technologies of text design and writing and printing techniques have added substantial meaning to textual messages.[19] All these histories, if not all written by historians, stress the importance of technologies for modes of human action and interaction, as well as the importance of the creation of knowledge and meaning.

Every contribution to this special issue connects to issues of technology, media and techniques in one way or another. Macnab, Grosvenor, and Myers deal explicitly with them by contrasting different technologies and media of production and

---

[13] Cf. Lawn and Grosvenor, eds., *Materialities of Schooling*.

[14] Cf. Marshall McLuhan and Quentin Fiore, *The Medium is the Message* (New York: Random House, 1967).

[15] André Leroi-Gourhan, *Le geste et la parole: Techniques et Langage* (Paris: Albin Michel, 1964).

[16] Norbert Elias, *Über den Prozeß der Zivilisation. Soziogenetische und psychogenetische Untersuchungen, Erster Band: Wandlungen des Verhaltens in den weltlichen Oberschichten des Abendlandes* (Basel: Verlag Haus zum Falken, 1939); Ibid., *Über den Prozeß der Zivilisation. Soziogenetische und psychogenetische Untersuchungen, Zweiter Band. Wandlungen der Gesellschaft. Entwurf einer Theorie der Zivilisation* (Basel: Verlag Haus zum Falken, 1939). Elias' work is published in English as *The Civilizing Process, Vol. I: The History of Manners* (Oxford: Blackwell, 1969) and *The Civilizing Process, Vol. II: State Formation and Civilization* (Oxford: Blackwell, 1982).

[17] Friedrich A. Kittler, *Aufschreibesysteme, 1800–1900* (Munich: Fink, 1985).

[18] Peter Burke, *A Social History of Knowledge: from Gutenberg to Diderot* (Cambridge: Polity Press, 2000).

[19] Cf. Chartier and Cavallo, *A History of Reading*.

display: in their article they reflect upon how the combined technologies of print and photography produced knowledge in two eras – one in which "production and publication were labour intensive, required specialist knowledge and training and so were relatively expensive" and one in which could be witnessed "the ability ... to reproduce text [and images] quickly and cheaply through mimeograph technology". It could be argued that while the technologies from both of the eras discussed in the article led to the production of media of low quality, this does not automatically imply that these media were less powerful vehicles of meaning-making. However, mimeograph technology as a more "democratic" means of production and display, through editing, enabled more collective authorship and thus broader participation. Roberts, in her account, points to photography (and to a minor extent also postcard production and lantern-slide projection) as a communication, surveillance and recording technology. In addition, she points to an important overlooked technology in a figurative sense – namely that of collecting and archiving, which involves processes of selection, ordering and cataloguing. Burke more implicitly touches upon technologies of production such as sculpting and painting, which can be connected to the arts and crafts movement and its discourse on educating aesthetic taste. Related to aesthetics and their conveyance of pedagogical rhetoric, the contribution of Parlevliet and Dekker brings to mind studies pointing out that drawings and prints, when reproduced in black and white, are abstractions of "real" family life.[20] Last but not least, Priem and Thyssen bring to the fore the easily overseen but powerful web of exhibition technologies: technologies of display (enlarging, cropping, etc.), montage, lighting and photo reproduction.

Translocation

All such technologies and media relied on the travel and circulation of knowledge in material and immaterial forms for their development, spread and adaptation. Whether they concern educational concepts, textbooks, exhibition sites, photo documentaries of children, ideas, visions and models of school decoration, children's poems, or charitable reports, as they circulate and cross borders – if only imagined ones[21] – their meaning changes.[22] The very times and spaces in which they appear and move add meanings that exceed any original intent or ontological nature. Production, diffusion and consumption (however fluid the boundaries between these processes may be) and the transforming of meaning that went along with any transfer involved are, therefore, issues central to all of the contributions to this special issue. The concept of translocation as a meaning-influencing factor is here intended to blur the boundaries between (naturalised) national borders, origins or belongings, essence and features, etc.[23] Put simply, it points to any kind of movement of texts,

---

[20] See, for example, the first chapter in Daston and Galison, *Objectivity*.
[21] Cf. Benedict Anderson, *Imagined Communities: Reflections on the Origin and Spread of Nationalism* (London: Verso, 1983).
[22] Cf. David Livingstone, "Keeping Knowledge in Site," *History of Education* 39, no. 6, 783.
[23] See Martin Lawn, "Awkward Knowledge: The Historian of Education and Cross-Border Circulations," in *Zirkulation und Transformation: Pädagogische Grenzüberschreitungen in historischer Perspektive*, ed. M. Caruso, T. Koinzer, C. Mayer and K. Priem (Cologne: Böhlau, forthcoming). See also Martin Lawn, ed., *An Atlantic Crossing? The Work of the International Examination Inquiry, its Researchers, Methods and Influence* (Oxford: Symposium, 2008).

images, objects, etc., separately or together, from space to space and time to time, and to the changes of meaning that can go along with that movement. Centring on what happens when works of art in visual, textual and material form travel, Rancière offers inspiration for the analysis of *how* processes of transfer affect such "travellers", *how* reception takes shape and *how* they form, question and undo existing ways of perceiving, judging and acting.[24] The travelling of knowledge, information and facts, objects, images, etc. may be thought of from this perspective as something that creates "dissensus",[25] thereby affecting bodies, minds and souls.

In the article by Macnab, Grosvenor, and Myers, which focuses on travelling images, it is shown that testimonies and descriptions worked rather to suppress any dissensus concerning the displacement of children from one country to another. The authors explicitly mention that this travelling went together with gaps that could have affected the integrity of what travelled and thus the truth or knowledge resulting from it. These gaps gave a convincing form and ethic of aid and humanitarianism to charitable activities, and it could be argued that protagonists of charitable organisations found in converging texts, numbers and photographs appropriate tools not to avoid silences but precisely to sustain them. In this case the transfer, with a lack of integrity on the receiving side, rather supported existing educational norms and practices imposed upon children of the poor, including transformations of their bodies and minds. By contrast, in the case of reading groups involving Liverpool black communities, gaps in the travel of facts were purposely and productively masked to create new conventions that moved "frontiers of the national imagination". As is mentioned by the authors, inspiration and resources were thereby drawn from people, ideas and sentiments crossing national and ideological borders. Roberts' contribution also explores paths of travel of different kinds of charitable reports and photographs, which acquire symbolic meaning across and in close association with the various "performative" spaces created by their production, collection and consumption. Among such spaces, she investigates contexts of propaganda and conservation sites (including memorial archives and libraries as well as files and binders connected in a network of other documents and images), which inevitably influence each other's interpretation. Importantly, Roberts' article also shows that space, circulation and transfer become inscribed in visual images through their reference to iconic models that transcend national or ideological boundaries. Parlevliet and Dekker similarly address issues of travel and reception while investigating processes of patterning, which involved the importation but also the adaptation of children's poems to fit children's everyday environments and their presumed age-specific interests within a context of patriotism. Burke's contribution, in turn, raises questions as to how educational ideals related to the democratisation of art as it travelled and materialised across countries, from commissioning reports to permanent features of school decoration and ex-pupils' spaces of biography. Travelling is also at the centre of the contribution by Priem and Thyssen: the constituents of the exhibition it explores, although coming from various cultural backgrounds, were orchestrated in a theatre of display that fit into the framework of a universalising project of American cultural diplomacy. However, the universal message of the show became disrupted by the local contexts to which it was transposed. Indeed, the show did not so much disrupt local contexts as it was challenged and undone by

---

[24] Rancière, *Dissensus*.
[25] Ibid.

them. Evidence of this kind undermines common assumptions underlying globalisation theories: all that travels generates dissensus as it becomes anchored in receiving contexts.

Heritage

Another important border is that between history and heritage, the crossing of which results in significant but so far neglected shifts in meaning. When texts, images, artefacts, sites, buildings, design and decoration features, or other remnants of the past, enter the realm of heritage from the realm of history, there occur important transformations of meaning. Heritage, rather than being "something" (be it a text, image, object, building, space or particular constellation of such elements), by definition is an "intangible" process or "performance"[26] through which certain aspects of the past, in order to become and remain recognised as such, need to be valued and re-valued in the light of what communities in the present (including scholars in the history of education) find important enough to pass on. While scholars like David Lowenthal have done much to delineate the boundaries between history and heritage, denouncing the perceived present "cult" of heritage and its supposedly "nostalgic" devotion to remnants of the past as a form of "false history",[27] heritage processes are by no means outside the domain of historians of education. Not only are they inextricably bound up with archival and museum practices; they are also connected to historiographical selection.

Historians of education themselves contribute to the valuing and revaluing of specific facets of the past – for example, by keeping attention focused on children's poems that moved from the sphere of the bourgeois homes of the Enlightenment to the didactic canon of the school up to the present (Parlevliet and Dekker). *Mutatis mutandis*, while disturbing what Eric Hobsbawm has called "invented traditions"[28] reiterated in textbooks omitting references to the slave trade and obscuring "rapacious British colonialism abroad [...] and [...] extensive domestic racism" (Macnab, Grosvenor, and Myers), historians of education also expose and co-construct "difficult" heritage.[29] Nevertheless, although in this domain, as in other disciplines, it is clear that "as social, political, and ideological conditions change, the meanings of the past can also change",[30] to date there has been less reflection upon how material and epistemic conditions also alter the meanings of the past. Such key material and epistemic conditions are involved in archive and museum practices and their

---

[26]Laurajane Smith, *All Heritage is Intangible: Critical Studies and Museums* (Kelpen-Oler: Reinwardt Academy, 2011), 9; Laurajane Smith, "The 'Doing' of Heritage: Heritage as Performance," in *Performing Heritage: Research, Practice and Innovation in Museum Theatre and Live Interpretation*, ed. A. Jackson and J. Kidd (Manchester: Manchester University Press, 2011), 69–81; Marilena Alivizatou, "Intangible Heritage and the Performance of Identity," in *Performing Heritage*, eds. Jackson and Kidd, 82–93.
[27]David Lowenthal, *The Heritage Crusade and the Spoils of History* (Cambridge: Cambridge University Press, 1998).
[28]Eric Hobsbawm, "Inventing Traditions," in *The Invention of Tradition*, ed. E. Hobsbawm and T. Ranger (Cambridge: Cambridge University Press, 1983), 1–2.
[29]William S. Logan and Keir Reeves, *Places of Pain and Shame: Dealing with Difficult Heritage* (London: Routledge, 2008).
[30]Paul A. Shackel, foreword to *Ethnographies and Archaeologies: Iterations of the Past* (Series: Cultural Heritage Studies), ed. Lena Mortensen and Julie Hollowell (Gainesville, FL: University Press of Florida, 2009).

curating technologies (collecting, selecting, cataloguing, displaying of exhibitions, etc.), many of which remain hidden[31] but still add to the formation of the collective memory and identity. The heritage construction accompanying these processes does not always remain excluded from view but is sometimes quite evident from institutions' names, as Roberts demonstrates in her account of charitable reports and photographs conserved at the International Brigade Memorial Archive and Marx Memorial Library in London. A remnant of the past that has developed from a "theatre of display" to a "theatre of memory"[32] is the *Family of Man* exhibition (Priem and Thyssen). Upon this transition from display to collective memory, the exhibit moved from a sphere of US cultural diplomacy and a flexible and modern set of exhibition design to the realm of Luxembourg's *lieux de mémoires*[33] and a high-brow artistic sphere.

Discussion: mobilising meaning-making

Interactions of text, imagery, material and so on and what is mediated through them over time in different places are at the heart of education and its didactical strategies of evidence, presentation and representation. Jointly constituting assemblies of representation within culturally loaded temporal–spatial settings, the words, pictures, things, places and so on assume meaning as they interact multimodally. As constellations, from a didactic–pedagogical perspective, they follow certain epistemologies directing how knowledge and "reality" should be perceived. On the one hand, the ideas, images, materials, sites and so on put on display in an educational framework already produce meaning by themselves, based as they are on a symbolic order of society. On the other, their arrangement and presentation also contribute to, and stimulate, meaning-making on the part of viewers or learners. Multimodality as such provides a research perspective that helps one to understand and analyse the complexities of meaning-making in educational settings.

Multiple modes mobilised in space and time require technologies and tools that, in turn, are contingent on cultural practices and techniques. The latter imply skills relevant for meaning-making and thus for societal participation, as the better they are learned, the more indicative they are of competence. This epistemological issue bound up with power thus far remains a neglected domain in the history of education. This is surprising, since the school has historically assumed (and still assumes) an important role in the teaching/learning of skills needed for the proliferation of technologies and facts that enable participation in the knowledge society's growing web of meaning-making. Technologies, requiring knowledge and offering different forms of access and agency in themselves, would need to be researched more profoundly, along with the processes of travel connected to them. Indeed, the development and spread of technologies – and thus of cultural practices and techniques – depends on travel but, inversely, travel also involves technologies in the most physical form. Translocation in the most material forms of travelling goes together with changes and losses of information which, in the long run, effect archival conditions.

---

[31] Ann L. Stoler, *Along the Archival Grain: Epistemic Anxieties and Colonial Common Sense* (Princeton University Press, 2010).
[32] Raphael Samuel, *Theatres of Memory: Past and Present in Contemporary Culture* (London: Verso, 1994).
[33] Pierre Nora, ed., *Les lieux de mémoire*, vol. 1–7 (Paris: Gallimard), 1984–92.

Gaps in the archive may indeed point to silences surrounding the human and non-human "networks" involved in travel and, through montage, may creatively be given meaning.[34] It is, however, necessary to consider the question of whether the silences occurred coincidentally or intentionally. Indeed, the transfer of knowledge and information has sometimes purposely lacked integrity across various education contexts (cf. Macnab, Grosvenor, and Myers), which complicates participation in meaning-making (for instance, in the construction of curricula). In each case, further analysis of *how* technologies and travel both mobilise meaning through different modes across spaces and realms could offer new perspectives for histories of education.

In sum, the mobilising of meaning assumes different qualities, which need to be reflected upon in the history of education in particular and education research in general. How does knowledge travel? In what ways is knowledge that travels and settles down in time and space capable of creating or suppressing dissensus affecting bodies, minds and souls? What technologies allow for participation by undoing hierarchies of meaning-making? These are just some of the questions this issue raises and offers for further inquiry.

---

[34]Catherine Burke and Ian Grosvenor, "The 'Body Parts' of the Victorian School Architect E.R. Robson or an Exploration of the Writing and Reading of a Life," in *Rethinking the History of Education: Transnational Perspectives on its Questions, Methods, and Knowledge*, ed. T. Popkewitz (New York: Palgrave, 2013), 201–20.

A poetic journey: the transfer and transformation of German strategies for moral education in late eighteenth-century Dutch poetry for children

Sanne Parlevliet and Jeroen J.H. Dekker

Department of Education, University of Groningen, The Netherlands

One of the most popular Dutch educational enlightenment authors was Hieronymus van Alphen. His three volumes of *Little Poems for Children* published in 1778 and 1782 were extremely successful, both in the Netherlands and abroad. Inspired by the German poets Christian Felix Weisse and Gottlob Wilhelm Burmann, Van Alphen brought about an expansion of educational space based on the integration of moral education in the spirit of the educational ideas of Locke, Rousseau and the Philanthropinists with poetical ideas and the nature of the child in both the content and the form of his poems. His poems were translated almost immediately into English, French and, surprisingly, as many of his poems were more or less adaptations of poems by Weisse and Burmann, into German too. Van Alphen's trump card was a reversal of former strategies of education: instead of pressing moral ideas upon the children from an adult point of view, he aimed at identification by (1) writing from the perspective of children, (2) situating the poems in the world of experience of children, (3) using a childlike style with a frolicking metre, rhyme scheme and prosody, and (4) combining text and images, so putting the moral message across visually and textually at the same time. In this paper, we follow the journey of poems for children as media for the cultural transmission of moral educational ideas from Germany to the Netherlands from the perspective of cultural transmission, moral literacy and educational space. We conclude that Van Alphen, with the combined power of text and image, successfully adopted and adapted former educational strategies, such as the moral poetics developed by his German predecessors Christian Felix Weisse and Gottlob Wilhelm Burmann. Taking their strategies on a poetic journey from Germany to the Netherlands, he not only transferred them, but transformed them as well. Van Alphen did so in a specific Dutch utilitarian way. His poems could be read for fun but were intended for learning. They were useful and entertaining at the same time, because he took the life and living environment of children into account, and particularly accounted for the concept of development as a distinguishing characteristic of the specific nature of the child with which child readers could identify.

Introduction: The father of Dutch children's literature

On 13 August 1775, a young Dutch solicitor lost his beloved wife. He was left with three small children, aged one, two and three years old.[1] Influenced by Enlightened educational philosophy,[2] he decided to raise them himself instead of putting out their education to a schoolmaster or a governess. However, in spite of the lively discourse and the many publications on the education of young children in the eighteenth century, which had been accelerating since Rousseau's publication of *Emile* in 1762, Children's books written in Dutch that were in line with Enlightened ideas and ideals were scarce, almost absent.[3] Shortly before the death of his wife, this solicitor had taken his first hesitant steps into the realm of poetry with some devotional miscellany. Shortly thereafter, he wrote a lamentation on her death.[4] Lacking appropriate, comprehensible reading material for his small children, he decided to expand his writing and wrote a small collection of poetry for young children, originally for his own.[5] The poems were published anonymously in 1778 and almost immediately followed by a second, non-anonymous volume, with a third a few years later. Both separately and bundled together, the volumes became bestsellers.[6] The name of the young Dutch solicitor was Hieronijmus van Alphen (1746–1803), and he would go down in history as the father of Dutch children's literature.[7] For more than 70 years, his poems were reprinted countless times and translated into many languages.[8] They were even set to music, and his poems echoed in those of his successors, both in form and in content.[9] During the last decades of the nineteenth century Van Alphen's poems were criticised. The children featuring in his poems were considered unrealistic. Critics asked for more realistic children, children who were a little bit naughty instead of primarily good. However, at the beginning of the twentieth century, the poems were rediscovered as an historical pedagogical monument by scholars and, at the same time, seen as providing a nostalgic memory

---

[1] P.J. Buijnsters, *Hieronymus van Alphen (1746–1803)* (Assen: Van Gorcum & Comp, 1973), 74; P.J. Buijnsters, "Nawoord" in *Hieronijmus van Alphen. Kleine Gedigten voor kinderen*, ed. P.J. Buijnsters (Amsterdam: Athenaeum – Polak & Van Gennep, 1998); Rene van Stipriaan, *Het volle leven* (Amsterdam: Prometheus, 2002), 304–5.
[2] Willeke Los, *Opvoeding tot mens en burger. Pedagogiek als cultuurkritiek in Nederland in de 18e eeuw* (Hilversum: Verloren, 2005).
[3] P.J. Buijnsters, "Nederlandse kinderboeken uit de achttiende eeuw," in *De hele Bibelebontse berg. De geschiedenis van het kinderboek in Nederland & Vlaanderen van de middeleeuwen tot heden*, ed. Nettie Heimeriks and Willem van Toorn (Amsterdam: Querido, 1989), 168–228; P.J. Buijnsters, "Nawoord'.
[4] Buijnsters, *Hieronymus*, 74–80.
[5] Buijnsters, "Nawoord," 174, 181–2; Buijnsters, "Nawoord," 64; Hieronijmus van Alphen, *Kleine Gedigten voor Kinderen*, ed. P.J. Buijnsters (Amsterdam: Athenaeum – Polak & Van Gennep, 1998), 117.
[6] Van Alphen wrote three volumes of *Little Poems for Children*. They were published in 1778, 1778 and 1782.
[7] Buijnsters, "Nawoord," 176; Buijnsters, "Nederlandse kinderboeken," 170.
[8] For example, in German in 1830/1831 (*Kleine Gedichte für Kinder des zarteren Alters*, translator unknown), in French in 1834 (*Petits poèmes à l'usage de l'enfance*, translated by A.J.T.A. Clavareau), in Malay in 1838 (*Babarapa panton bagi'ânakh p. terkârang dâlam bahâsa Wolanda 'awleh Hieronomus van Alphen*, translated by G. Hejmering) and in English in 1856 (*Poetry for children*, translated by F.J. Millard).
[9] For example, in the poems of the Dutch poets Pieter 't Hoen, Hendrik Riemsnijder and Dirk Onderwater.

of the past on the part of the general public.[10] This resulted in many more reprints and the poems' inclusion in literary histories – especially school books on literature – in which we can find some of them even today.[11] Over time, the poems have been and continue to be used in education, and so have been transformed and reframed in several ways.[12]

Van Alphen represents an internationally acclaimed children's literary turn.[13] He brought the international pedagogical legacy of Locke, Rousseau and his Dutch predecessors such as Jacob Cats together with the then contemporary Enlightened body of pedagogical thought of the Philanthropinists to produce a new form of children's poetry. In this article, we will demonstrate how he adapted the poetic strategies of two German Philanthropinist poets to the cultural context of Dutch Enlightenment.

The Netherlands did not lack books for children in the eighteenth century. Abecedariums, the Proverbs and children's catechisms were read in schools. Protestant textbooks based on the Bible and intended for school or home education had long been present. And although the view is common that the eighteenth century lacked books specifically intended for children in which imagination ruled, books that could be read primarily for fun, the eighteenth century knew many examples of amusing picture books with movable images, scrapbooks, fairy-tale volumes and gift books. There was also nonfiction intended for children: almanacs, poems and plays.[14] Moreover, light reading for young and old was sold on many street corners and in stationers' shops, such as chap books with old folk-tales, Aesop's fables, travel accounts, puzzle books, penny dreadfuls and penny picture prints.[15]

Amidst this abundance of literature for children, how did Hieronijmus van Alphen acquire the designation of father, often even founder, of Dutch children's literature? The answer lies in his transformation of previous educational strategies, the strategies of Dutch moral poetry from the seventeenth and early eighteenth centuries[16] and the strategies he found in German moral poetry for children. In this article, we will demonstrate the latter. First, we will address the utilitarian context of the Dutch Enlightenment in which van Alphen was operating. Then we will present the elements van Alphen adopted from his German examples, Christian Felix Weisse and Gottlob Wilhelm Burmann, and how he adapted them to the strategies and style

---

[10] Buijnsters, "Nawoord," 190–2; L.J.Th. Wirth, *Een eeuw kinderpoëzie 1778–1878* (Groningen, The Hague: J.B. Wolters" U.M. 1926).

[11] In particular, "The Plum Tree" (De pruimenboom) has become part of the collective memory of The Netherlands and Flanders. See for example the secondary school textbook by H.J.M.F. Lodewick, *Literatuurgeschiedenis. Bloemlezing*, vol. 1 ('s- Hertogenbosch: L.C.G. Malmberg, 1960 or 1958), pp. 246–7.

[12] An illustration of such very recent transformation or reframing – of which more later – can be found on http://www.gedichtendag.com/2010/documenten/lessuggesties/basis_2010.pdf (accessed August 11, 2013).

[13] Py, G., *Rousseau et les éducateurs. Etude sur la fortune des idées pédagogiques de Jean-Jacques Rousseau en France et en Europe au XVIIIe siècle* (Oxford: Voltaire Foundation, 1997).

[14] P.J. Buijnsters and Leontine Buijnsters-Smets, *Bibliografie van Nederlandse school- en kinderboeken 1700-1800* (Zwolle: Waanders, 1997).

[15] Buijnsters, "Nawoord," 176–7.

[16] Cf. J.J.H. Dekker, "Moral Literacy. The Pleasure of Learning How to Become Decent Adults and Good Parents in the Dutch Republic in the Seventeenth Century,' *Paedagogica Historica* 44 (2008): 135–49.

of moral poetry that made him so successful and famous in the late eighteenth, nineteenth and even twentieth centuries.

Fairy tales or useful stories? Utilitarianism and the birth of Enlightened educational poetry

The abundance of available books that could be read primarily for fun did not meet the requirements of Dutch Enlightened educational culture in the late eighteenth century, which was utilitarian: reading for children should always be useful. Enlightened pedagogues saw harm in "foolish fairy tales".[17] Consequently, truly Enlightened parents did not want their children to read merely for fun and excitement, and therefore rejected chap books and other cheap or fantastic reading material.[18] They wanted books for children to increase children's knowledge and virtue, which were greatly favoured over pleasure – a tendency prevailing in Dutch moral educational literature from the seventeenth century onward.[19] Nevertheless, pleasure in reading was not rejected altogether. Enlightened pedagogical poetics built on Locke's idea of pleasure as a pedagogical device. Van Alphen's merit was his understanding that integrating children as characters – in van Alphen's case, bourgeois children of both sexes – in the moral lessons would increase children's pleasure in reading, as we will demonstrate in the next section. Moreover, van Alphen recognised the power of combining text and image for children reading or being read the poems. Therefore, he wanted very much for the poems to be used together with illustrations, and so for the text and illustrations to be published together. Although his publisher did not immediately see the good of it, van Alphen was able to announce illustrations in the preface of his second volume, *Vervolg der kleine gedigten voor kinderen* [Sequel to Little Poems for Children]. Initially, the illustrations were published apart from the text – the publisher was slow to be convinced of their value – but could and would, as van Alphen intended, be bound with the poems, which was not unusual in the eighteenth century.[20] Their combination with illustrations by Jacobus Buijs (1724–1801) added much to the popularity of the poems.[21] In visualising his moral messages with images, van Alphen followed the strategy of Jacob Cats, the famous and popular seventeenth-century moralist and author of bestselling child-rearing advisory books. But van Alphen's representational strategy differed immensely from that of his seventeenth-century predecessor. While the images accompanying Cats' moral texts gave symbolic representations of the recommended virtue or mode of behaviour, Buijs' illustrations for van Alphen's

---

[17] Betje Wolff, *Proeve over de opvoeding, aan de Nederlandsche moeders* (Amsterdam: Johannes Allart, 1779), 83.
[18] Arianne Baggerman and Rudolf Dekker, *Het dagboek van Otto van Eck* (Hilversum: Verloren, 1998); Arianne Baggerman and Rudolf Dekker, *Kind van de toekomst. De wondere wereld van Otto van Eck* (Amsterdam: Wereldbibliotheek, 2005).
[19] Jeroen J.H. Dekker, *Het verlangen naar opvoeden. ver de groei van de pedagogische ruimte in Nederland sinds de Gouden Eeuw tot omstreeks 1900* (Amsterdam: Bert Bakker, 2006), 129–31; for examples of Dutch emblematic literature see John Manning, Karel Porteman, and Marc van Vaeck, eds., *The Emblem Tradition and the Low Countries* (Turnhout: Brepols, 1999).
[20] Buijnsters, "Nawoord,' 188.
[21] Buijnsters, "Nawoord,' 186, 189–190, 192–193.

poems intended to foster a direct insight into the primary moral development addressed in the text of the poem.[22] They were intended to make clear at a quick glance what the message was about, while the brief poem completed the message of the image. As a result, children who could not yet read would also get the message immediately, or so van Alphen thought. They would not need any knowledge of symbols or skills in interpreting symbolic images, as was the case with the emblems by Cats. They were expected to grasp the content of the poem immediately by looking at its concrete visual "translation". An excellent example of this is the image for the poem "Joyful Learning" (see Figure 1), which will be discussed further below.

Van Alphen's poems fitted the enlightened idea of moral education in service of nation building. Enlightened Protestant citizens promoted patriotism and citizenship for all, which meant transforming the decentralised, previously flourishing but now economically stagnating Dutch Republic into a centrally governed nation state. They strove for an inclusive and national citizenship, in contrast to the prevailing exclusive and locally based citizenship of the Dutch Republic. Literacy for all, including both the practice of reading and writing and acting according to the propounded virtues (in other words, moral literacy), was considered necessary for that universal citizenship. Citizenship for all first meant literacy for all, for both boys and girls. Literacy for all meant, in turn, education for all.[23]

Van Alphen was caught by "the spark of patriotic fire" in the late 1770s and became convinced that a sense of patriotism would give his languishing country new energy. The Dutch people would regain their strength when patriotism spread throughout the population.[24] Apparently, the patriotic spark could not be lit early enough: in a poem entitled "The Love for the Fatherland",[25] Van Alphen introduced his young readers to his new ideal:

Although I am only a Child,

My Fatherland is most loved by me

[...]

And once I become a man,

---

[22] See Jeroen Jansen, "The Emblem Theory and Audience of Jacob Cats,' in *The Emblem Tradition and the Low Countries*, ed. Manning et al., 227–42; Jeroen J.H. Dekker, "Beauty and Simplicity. The Power of Fine Art in Moral Teaching on Education in 17th Century Holland," *Journal of Family History. Studies in Family, Kinship, and Demography* 34, no. 2 (2009): 166–88; Dekker, "Moral Literacy," 135–49; Dekker, *Het verlangen naar opvoeden*, 65–6.

[23] Dekker, "Moral Literacy," 137–40; J.J.H. Dekker, "From Imaginations To Realities: The Transformation Of Enlightenment Pedagogical Illusions Of The Dutch Republic Into Late 19th-Century Realities Of The Dutch Monarchy," in *Schooling and the Making Of Citizens in the Long Nineteenth Century: Comparative Visions*, ed. D. Tröhler, T. Popkowitz, and D. Labaree (New York/London: Routledge, 2011), 50–69.

[24] Preface by Van Alphen to the translation of Thomas Abbt's *Vom Verdienste* by G.T. van Paddenburg (1777).

[25] We have provided with a functional English translation of all of the Dutch poems and their titles. More free translations of the poems can be found in Poetry for children by Hieronymus van Alphen; translated into English verse by F.J. Millard (London: Partridge & Co., 1856).

MODES AND MEANING: DISPLAYS OF EVIDENCE IN EDUCATION

I will be as useful to my country as I can.[26]

In the drawing accompanying this poem, a Dutch boy stands before a pillar incorporating the Dutch Lion, thus indicating his patriotism and the promise that, with the support of national education, he will be useful to his country.[27]

After Locke's encouragement of appreciation of children's play, it was often used in reading material as something adults could take pleasure in. Seeing children play was perceived to be entertaining and had been used to teach moral lessons.[28] As did all Enlightenment-inspired educational writers, van Alphen systematically linked playing to learning in his texts. However, he did not address adults, but children themselves. Enlightened education claimed that children's play always had to be focused on its utility and to be aimed at improving behaviour, gaining knowledge or learning virtues. Playing was not for pleasure alone but had to serve the learning process. Van Alphen's poems were written in function of this ideal, which was picked up by other writers for children. For example, in his *Vaderlandsch A-B Boek voor de Nederlandsche Jeugd* [*National Abecedarium for Dutch Youth*], the Dutch writer Johan Hendrik Swildens (1781) went so far as to link children's play directly with professions that would be undertaken in the future. In emphasising that children's play should contribute to the creation of sensible and useful citizens, he agreed with van Alphen's utilitarian approach to children's play.[29]

Accordingly, van Alphen adhered to the Enlightened creed that developing one's head entailed developing one's heart. According to Enlightenment pedagogy, children had to be taught that becoming complete citizens without sufficient knowledge was impossible. Ignorance deprived one of being a full human being.[30] Although van Alphen never mentioned the social value of the moral virtues he praises, his poems fit Enlightenment norms and values perfectly. For example, van Alphen's famous poem entitled "Joyful Learning" is an expression of the idea of the interweaving of playing and learning. A boy, sitting behind his desk with a quill in his hand – a symbol of learning – points to his toys, a peg top and a hoop, symbolising an inclination to play, and makes the following famous declaration:

> My playing is learning, my learning is playing,
>> So why should learning be boring?
>> Reading and writing are fun.
>> I will swap my top and hoop for books;
>> I will pass my time with my prints,

---

[26]"Al ben ik maar een kind,/Tog wordt mijn Vaderland van mij op 't hoogst bemind; /[...]/ En, worde ik eens een man,/Zo nuttig zijn voor 't land, als ik maar wezen kan" (Van Alphen, *Kleine Gedigten*, 129).
[27]Cf. N.C.F. van Sas, *De metamorfose van Nederland* (Amsterdam: Amsterdam University Press, 2004), 69–171; N.C.F. van Sas, "De vaderlandse imperatief," in *Vaderland: een geschiedenis van de vijftiende eeuw tot 1940* (Amsterdam: Amsterdam University Press, 1999), 275–308.
[28]Nelleke Bakker, Jan Noordman, and Marjoke Rietveld-Van Wingerden, *Vijf eeuwen opvoeden in Nederland: idee en praktijk 1500–2000* (Assen: Koninklijke Van Gorcum, 2006).
[29]Joost Kloek and Wijnand Mijnhardt, *1800 – Blauwdrukken voor een samenleving* (Den Haag: SDU Uitgevers, 2001), 292; Van Sas, *De metamorfose*, 74–75, 106–107.
[30]Buijnsters, "Nawoord," 183.

Wisdom and virtues are what I long for.[31]

The image accompanying this poem (see Figure 1) had to make clear immediately what was going on. The dilemma of having to choose between learning and play was presented by the symbols of learning, such as the desk and the quill, and the symbols of playing, the boy's toys. Even very young children were intended to grasp the meaning of the poem immediately by looking at the image. All of the poems were accompanied by images that were intended to convey the meaning of the poems directly. As this particular poem was very short, the image was designed to reflect all the elements of the text. Images that accompanied the longer poems could not possibly refer to all elements of the poems and so focused mostly on the moral struggle that arose from the moral dilemmas presented to the child.

Van Alphen's emphasis, in this poem, on the pleasant side of learning for young children was unique to his generation. He followed the older example of Jacob Cats, the successful author of best- and long-selling books on education and marriage in the seventeenth century. Cats was a moralist and a writer of emblem books, who also combined teaching the virtues with entertainment. However, he intended his work for adult readers.[32] Cats' works, probably the most read books in the region in the seventeenth century apart from the Bible and the fourteenth-century *De Imitatione Christi* by Thomas à Kempis, remained popular throughout the eighteenth century. The writer Rhijnvis Feith (1753–1824), editor of a new edition of Cats' collected works, considered them as "handbooks for the youth", as "really Dutch", and described them in terms of superlatives such as "the sanctuary".[33] The enduring popularity of Cats' works was a result of Rhijnvis Feith, like his contemporaries, interpreting them in the light of modern Enlightenment citizenship ideals. As a result, Cats' seventeenth-century emblematic books became "the bible of the new citizen ideal" – an ideal that Cats himself, living and writing in seventeenth-century Reformation Europe, could never even have conceived.[34]

While the combination of learning and play was a frequent topic in moralistic Dutch literature, the late eighteenth-century educational discourse was specific in being explicitly didactic, emphasising learning over play, which was behaviour to be avoided by children.[35] In this context, "Joyful Learning" and van Alphen's other poems became very popular. They were read by children and by parents who read

---

[31] "Mijn speelen is leeren, mijn leeren is speelen,/En waarom zou mij dan het leeren verveelen?/Het leezen en schrijven verschaft mij vermaak/'t Is wijsheid, "t zijn deugden, naar welke ik haak./Ik wil in mijn prenten mijn tijdverdrijf zoeken,/Mijn hoepel, mijn priktol verruil ik voor boeken" (Van Alphen, *Kleine Gedigten*, 25).

[32] J.J.H. Dekker, "Woord en beeld: Jacob Cats en de pedagogische cultuuroverdracht in de zeventiende eeuw', in J.W. Steutel, D. J. de Ruyter, and S. Miedema, eds., *De gereformeerden en hun vormingsoffensief door de eeuwen heen* (Zoetermeer: Meinema, 2009), 47–65; Dekker, "Moral Literacy'; Dekker, "Beauty and Simplicity,' 166–88.

[33] J. Kloek and W. Mijnhardt, "De verlichte burger," in *Burger*, ed. J. Kloek and K. Tilmans (Amsterdam: Amsterdam University Press, 2002), 166–7.

[34] Kloek & Mijnhardt, "De verlichte burger," in *Burger*, ed. Kloek and Tilmans, 166–167; Kloek and Mijnhardt, *1800*, 584; Kloek and Tilmans, "Inleiding," in *Burger*, ed Kloek and Tilmans, 9–10; Prak Maarten, *Gouden Eeuw. Het raadsel van de Republiek* (Nijmegen: SUN, 2002), 17.

[35] See Van Alphen, *Kleine Gedigten*, 29.

MODES AND MEANING: DISPLAYS OF EVIDENCE IN EDUCATION

Figure 1. Hieronijmus Van Alphen, Joyful Learning [Het vrolijke leren]. From: Hieronijmus van Alphen, Kleine gedichten voor kinderen (Rare Books Department, University Library, University of Groningen, 2L 1579) (Utrecht: Wed. J. van Terveen en Zoon, 1787), pp. 10–11.

them to their children, as Willem van den Hull (1778–1858) described in his autobiography and Otto van Eck (1780–1798) in his diary.[36] Implicitly, van Alphen

---

[36]Jacques Dane, "Zwarigheid voor het kinderverstand. De *Kleine Gedichten* van Van Alphen," *NRC Handelsblad*, August 28, 1998, 7; Arianne Baggerman and Rudolf Dekker, *Child of the Enlightenment. Revolutionary Europe Reflected in a Boyhood Diary.* (Leiden/Boston: Brill, 2009; originally published in Dutch in 2005, trans. Diane Webb).

even added moral messages for parents by not only telling children how to behave, think and reason as growing Enlightened citizens, but also telling parents how to raise their children in an Enlightened way.

Adding to their popularity was the omission of explicit reference to religious dogmas. The result was that the poems featured the general form of Christianity that characterised Dutch Enlightenment.[37] Described as the "laudable Enlightenment Pedagogics by Hieronijmus van Alphen", the poems were given a central place on the *General List of Books for Primary Schools in the Northern Provinces of the Kingdom of the Netherlands* in 1815, which was drawn up with the educational ambition of determining what Dutch children should read and what they should not. It was a typical Enlightenment-based list that advised schoolteachers of all denominations what stories should be read by their pupils, omitting everything supernatural, such as fantastic reading material or tales of Catholic saints, while recommending useful reading material.[38]

From the publication of his first volume onward, van Alphen was praised for his innovation of moral literature up until the second half of the nineteenth century,[39] studied for his innovative pedagogical approach of the child from the beginning of the twentieth century onward,[40] reviled for presenting ideal, virtuous cardboard children from the 1930s onward,[41] and rediscovered in the 1990s as one of the international poets to succeed best in writing poetry with a childlike nature.[42] In historical pedagogical studies and studies on the history of children's literature, van

---

[37] Dekker, *Het verlangen*, 188; Kloek and Mijnhardt, *1800*.

[38] P.J. Buijnsters and Leontine Buijnsters-Smets, *Lust en leering. De geschiedenis van het Nederlandse kinderboek in de negentiende eeuw* (Zwolle: Waanders, 2001), 46–7; P.J. Buijnsters, "Het eeuwenoude storiegoed," in *De mondige jeugdliteratuur*, ed. Piet Mooren, Jeanne Kurvers, and Helma van Lierop-Debrauwer (Leidschendam: Biblion Uitgeverij, 2004), 39–40; cf. J.J.H. Dekker, *Educational Ambitions in History. Childhood and Education in an Expanding Educational Space from the Seventeenth to the Twentieth Century* (Frankfurt am Main: Peter Lang, 2010), 78–9.

[39] Een Cosmopoliet, *Tafreel van de zeden, opvoeding, geleerdheid, smaak, en verlichting, in het voormalig gewest van Holland* (Amsterdam: Matthijs Schalekamp, 1798); Donker Curtius, "Beschouwing van de Kleine Gedichten voor Kinderen van wijlen Mr. Hieronijmus van Alphen" in *Nieuwe bijdragen ter bevordering van het onderwijs en de opvoeding II* (1827), 772–89; Van Harderwijk, *Proeve eener Lofrede op Mr. H. van Alphen* (1829); J.T. Bodel Hijenhuis, *Lofrede op Mr. H. van Alphen* (1829); J. Clarisse, Over Hieronymus van Alphen als dichter en kinderdichter. Twee voorlezingen in De Fakkel (1831-1832); A. van Vloten, "Van Alphens kindergedichten" in *Algemeene Konst- en Letterbode* (1857), 99.

[40] Cf. H. Pomes, *Over Van Alphens kindergedichtjes* (Rotterdam: W.L. & J. Brusse, 1908); P.L. van Eck, "Van Alphen als kinderdichter," *Groot-Nederland* (1908), 213–38; L.J.T. Wirth, *Een eeuw kinderpoëzie 1778–1878* (Groningen/Den Haag: J.B. Wolters, 1925); P.L. van Eck, "Van Alphen in 't Duits," *Levende talen 127* (1943), 265–68; W. van Doorn, "Van Alphen in 't Engels," *Levende talen 127* (1943), 263–5; P.J. Buijnsters, *Hieronymus van Alphen (1746–1803)* (Assen: Van Gorcum, 1973); P.J. Buijnsters "Nawoord" in *Hieronijmus van Alphen, Kleine gedigten voor kinderen* (Amsterdam: Athenaeum – Polak & Van Gennep, 1998).

[41] Cf. Hildebrand, "Kinderrampen," in *Camera Obscura* (Haarlem: Erven F. Bohn, 1839); P.A. de Genestet, De *Sint-Nikolaasavond* (Zwolle: Tjeenk Willink, 1903 [1849]); P.A. de Genestet, *Over kinderpoezy* (Gebroeders Kraay, Amsterdam z.j. [1858]); Nicolaas Beets, "Over kinderboeken. Gesprek met Crito," in *Verscheidenheden, meest op letterkundig gebied III*, ed. Nicolaas Beets (De erven F. Bohn, Haarlem, 1867), 1–66.

[42] Willem Wilmink, "Hieronymus van Alphen," in *Wat ik heb gevonden, je raadt het nooit* (Amsterdam: Bakker, 1990).

Alphen has often been described as the first children's writer to write poems that were actually attractive for children, because he had an appreciation of the child and the childlike.

This attractiveness has been attributed to the incorporation of the child's living environment and the attractive poetic style. In the following we will demonstrate another crucial, innovative element of van Alphen's children's poetry: his incorporation of the concept of development as characteristic of growing children, which counters accusations of unchildlikeness. We will show how van Alphen aimed more at identification than did his German predecessors Weisse and Burmann, and how he did this by means of familiarity and recognition. Van Alphen patterned his poems on those by Weisse and Burmann and so took the perspective of children into account, whereas many books for children at that time were characterised by pressing moral ideas upon children from an adult point of view. But much more than Weisse and Burmann, van Alphen gave his paper children a voice that was not a mere mouthpiece of adult ideas but reflected a more childlike view. He was unique in attempting to engage with the world of the child by writing about the tension between the child's heart and head and depicting development as a distinctive feature of childhood, thereby representing the process of education instead of focusing solely on the ideal results of education.

In the following, we shall demonstrate four decisive aspects of van Alphen's transformation of the child orientation he adopted from Weisse and Burmann: (1) he changed the child orientation by giving specific attention to development as a key characteristic whereby he realised an intensified orientation towards the developing child, both male and female, instead of towards an already morally well-developed child; (2) more specifically than Weisse and Burmann, van Alphen situated, in both texts and illustrations, most of his moral messages explicitly within the nuclear family, which constituted the most promising educational space for the Enlightened bourgeois of the Netherlands;[43] (3) he assigned the role of nature in his poems differently from Weisse and Burmann; and (4) he also dealt with religion differently.

A poetic journey through space: adopting and transforming German examples

The influence of Christian Felix Weisse (1726–1804) and Gottlob Wilhelm Burmann (1737–1805) was described by van Alphen himself in the preface to his first volume of children's poetry: he had "read the German *Lieder für Kinder* [*Songs for Children*] by Weisse and the *Kleine Lieder für kleine Madchën und Jünglinge* [*Little Songs for Little Girls and Boys*] by G.W. Burmann with much pleasure, and they often showed him the way…". [44] Van Alphen probably became acquainted with Weisse's and Burmann's work because he kept up with German

---

[43]Cf. J.F. Martinet, Huisboek voor vaderlandsche huisgezinnen (Amsterdam: Johannes Allart, 1803 or 1793); W. de Vos, "Verhandeling over het huwelijk,' *Verhandelingen van het genootschap Floreant Liberales Artes* 1 (1791).

[44]"(…) en dat hij de Hoogduitsche *Lieder für Kinder* van Weisse en de *Kleine Lieder für kleine Mädchen und Jünglinge* van G.W. Burmann, met zeer veel genoegen, gelezen heeft (…)" (Van Alphen, *Kleine Gedigten*, 11). Burmann is also spelled as Bormann.

literature, art, theology and philosophy. In a preface to the Dutch translation of *Vom Verdienste* of Thomas Abbt by Van Paddenburg, van Alphen exclaimed: "Let us emulate Germany! How they have progressed in the field of the *belles lettres* in the past thirty years!"[45]

Moreover, classic texts written by Philanthropinists such as Joachim Heinrich Campe (1746–1818) and Christian Gotthilf Salzmann (1744–1811) – it was less the case with texts by Johann Bernhard Basedow (1724–1790) – were quickly translated into Dutch.[46] Those German *Philanthropinists*, in particular Basedow and Campe, became a source of inspiration for Dutch Enlightenment thinkers through the design and inauguration of their educational experiment, the *Philanthropium*, which was founded in Dessau in 1774.[47] As the late eighteenth-century Dutch educational culture was more pragmatic than philosophical and less interested in the radical philosophical experiments so characteristic of *Émile*, Dutch culture was focused on proven practical ways of educating children in the virtues of good citizenship. Those methods were to be seen at Dessau and not in Rousseau's *Émile*.[48] Salzmann, whose moral books were of special interest to the morally oriented Dutch educational culture and were reprinted several times, was of the opinion that children could be educated in the virtues most efficiently by having them read books about virtuous men and women.[49] Hie-

---

[45] Cited from Buijnsters, *Hieronymus*, 96.

[46] Campe, one of the first professional German authors of children's books, published *Robinson der Jüngere* in 1799–1780, a moralising version of Defoe's original work and the only book Rousseau permitted Émile to read. Cf. S. Parlevliet, *Meesterwerken met ezelsoren. Bewerkingen van literaire klassiekers voor kinderen 1850-1950* (Hilversum: Verloren, 2009), 96; Aubrey Rosenberg, "Rousseau's Emile: The Nature and Purpose of Education," in *The Educational Legacy of Romanticism*, ed. John Willinsky (Waterloo, Ontario: Wilifred Laurier University Press, 1990), 20; Buijnsters and Buijnsters-Smets, *Lust en leering*, 11–12; n. 5 on p. 424 for the daily readings by Otto van Eck, then 10 years old, from "Basedows *Elementarwerk*" in a French translation; Baggerman and Dekker, *Het dagboek*, 50; Marjoke Rietveld-van Wingerden, *Voor de lieve kleinen. Het jeugdtijdschrift in Nederland 1757-1942* (Den Haag: Nederlands Bibliotheek en Lektuur centrum, 1992).

[47] Buijnsters and Buijnsters-Smets, *Lust en leering*, 10; Marcel Grandière, *L'idéal pédagogique en France au dix-huitieme siecle* (Oxford: Voltaire Foundation, 1998); Gilbert Py, *Rousseau et les éducateurs. Étude sur la fortune des idées pédagogique de Jean-Jacques Rousseau en France et en Europe au XVIIIe siècle* (Oxford: Voltaire Foundation, 1997); Rosenberg, "Rousseau's Emile"; Hans van Crombrugge, "Emile en Sophie wisselen boeken uit. Lectuur en meisjesopvoeding bij Rousseau," *Pedagogiek* 21 (2001), 68–78; Hans van Crombrugge, "Rousseau on family and education," *Paedagogica Historica* 31 (1995), 445–80.

[48] Walter Gobbers, *Jean-Jacques Rousseau in Holland. Een onderzoek naar de invloed van de mens en het werk* (Gent, 1963). An exception was the Rousseau adherent Johannes Kneppelhout (1814–1885); cf. Jacques Dane, "'Meer en meer paedagoog geworden.' Opvoeding rondom Johannes Kneppelhout," *De negentiende eeuw* 26 (2002), 199–217.

[49] Cf. Buijnsters and Buijnsters-Smets, *Lust en leering*, 23–5; Parlevliet, *Meesterwerken*; Nelleke Bakker, Hans van Crombrugge, and Marjoke Rietveld-van Wingerden, eds., *Naar Duits model. De receptie van Duitse pedagogische idealen uit de vroege negentiende eeuw* (Assen: Koninklijke Van Gorcum, 2003). The already mentioned Swildens was a convinced adherent of the Philanthropinists; his *Vaderlandsch A-B boek* was inspired by Salzmann's texts. He filled his book with examples of the social virtues that should be learned by the youth to help them become good citizens and patriots. In 1813, Swildens published his Booklet on Virtues [*Deugden-boekje*], inspired by Campe. Cf. Van Sas, *De metamorfose*, 106–7; Jaap ter Linden, *A is een Aapje. Opstellen over ABC-boeken van de vijftiende eeuw tot heden* (Amsterdam: Querido, 1995).

ronijmus van Alphen, as we saw above, was one of the main representatives of that new educational culture in the Netherlands, so it was no wonder that he looked at German examples in the Philanthropinist tradition for his poetry and that he discovered the poems by Weisse and Burmann.

Both Weisse and Burmann wrote other things as well, but they were especially popular for their children's poems in Germany because these were embraced by the Philanthropinist educators. The transfer of Weisse's *Lieder für Kinder* (1767) and Burmann's *Kleine Lieder für kleine Mädchen und Jünglinge* (1777) to the Netherlands must have benefited from this lively exchange of educational ideas. Weisse also received much public favour for his weekly magazine for children, *Der Kinderfreund* [*The Children's Friend*] (1776–1782), which was read in many countries. Moreover, Weisse was one of the first German poets who dedicated his pen exclusively to children. His motivation was similar to Van Alphen's although it was prompted by a more cheerful event: he started writing for his own children shortly after he became a father himself. His autobiography (1806) reads:

> Im Jahre 1765 war Weisse zum erstenmal Vater geworden. Seine innige Freude darüber und die Anhänglichkeit an das kleine Geschöpf ward Ursache, dass er oftmals in der Nähe desselben war und die abgeschmackten Lieder der Amme und Kinderwärterin singen hörte. Das brachte ihn auf den Entschluss, kleine moralische Lieder für Kinder zu dichten.[50]

Weisse's poems instantly fell on the fertile ground of Philanthropinist ideology. He published his volume in the period during which German education had started to be severely criticised by adherents of rationalism and Enlightened education, just before Basedow's cry of distress in 1768 in *Vorstellung an Menschenfreunde und vermögende Männer über Schulen, Studien und ihren Einfluss in die öffentliche Wohlfahrt* [*Proposal to Philanthropinists and Wealthy Men about Schools, Studies and their Influence on Common Prosperity*]. Weisse explicitly sympathised with the Philanthropinist movement. He intended his poems to impart virtue to children, which suited the Philanthropinists' adaptation of Rousseau's philosophy and Enlightened bourgeois ideology for education. The poems promoted virtues such as diligence, the sense of duty, compassion, helpfulness, modesty, gratitude and love for their parents and siblings in order to prepare children to become useful and happy citizens. The form Weisse chose for his poems also suited Basedow's idea of pleasure in learning and was an entirely new form of poetry, attractive and simple. The texts were singable, easy accessible and understandable for the young, and written entirely in the Enlightened spirit of the age. Through their immediate popularity Weisse contributed greatly to the emancipation, spread and popularisation of Enlightened bourgeois ideology.[51]

Burmann also wrote his poems explicitly for children and published a volume of fables as well, which was not explicitly meant for children but can be categorised as

---

[50] "In 1765 Weisse became a father. His great joy and affection for the little creature urged him to stay close so that he often heard the flavourless songs sung by the wet nurse and the nanny. This made him decide to compose short moral songs for children." Cited from Theodor Brüggemann, *Handbuch zur Kinder- und Jugendliteratur von 1750 bis 1800* (Stuttgart: Metzler, 1982), 87.

[51] Schmidt, 1974, cited in Brüggemann, *Handbuch*, 93.

moral didactical poetry of the sort that was much recommended for the young in eighteenth-century bourgeois society.[52] He was also a journalist and a musician, and many of his children's poems were accompanied by a melody for singing. His poems and occasional poems, songs and epigrams were popular during the 1760s and 1770s. Later on, he became known as somewhat eccentric, and his work was characterised by Kotzebue as "Bizarrerie" [extravagance].[53] Such an experimental work was his *Gedichte ohne den Buchstabe R* [*Poems Without the Letter R*] (1788), in which he omitted the letter R completely to find out if the German language would be more pleasant without it.[54] Nevertheless, he is remembered first and foremost for his children's poetry.

Van Alphen adapted seven poems by Weisse and four by Burmann directly.[55] However, all his other poems are suffused with the same Enlightened bourgeois spirit, and many of them deal with the same concepts, ideas and ideals. He partly adopted Weisse's and Burmann's poetic contents and styles, but he also transformed them substantially by orienting them to the child, by situating the moral messages almost unexceptionally in the nuclear family and by modifying the role of nature and religion. The following deals with the way in which van Alphen's poems correspond to those of his sources of inspiration and how the journey from Germany to the Netherlands changed them.

Children's perspectives

One of the defining elements Van Alphen adopted from Weisse and Burmann is the incorporation of children's perspectives in his poems. They literally gave children a voice by making them the subject – the lyrical I – in many poems:[56] "Mein Hundchen ist ein gutes Thier;/So bald ich rufe, folgt es mir";[57] "Fromm, fromm will ich auf Erden seyn,/Und als ein Knabe schon/Mich meines nahen Gottes freun;/ Groß durch Religion".[58] Children's play and toys also appear next to, or in favour of, the moral message, such as dolls and a sword in Burmann's "An die Puppen" [To the Dolls] and "Der Degen" [The Sword], and a top, a snowman and a house of cards in Weisse's "Der Krausel" (The top), "Der Schneeman" [The Snowman] and "Das Kartenhäuschen" [The House of Cards]. The child's perception is nicely put

---

[52] Brüggemann, *Handbuch*, 1298.
[53] Hermann Palm, "Burmann, Gottlob Wilhelm," in *Allgemeine Deutsche Biographie, herausgegeben von der Historischen Kommission bei der Bayerischen Akademie der Wissenschaften* 3 (1876), 627–8.
[54] Karl Heinrich Jördens, *Denkwürdigkeiten, Charakterzüge und Anekdoten aus dem Leben der vorzüglichsten deutschen Dichter* 1 (Leipzig, 1812), 66–82.
[55] Buijnsters, "Nawoord," 181–2; H. Pomes, *Over Van Alphen's kindergedichtjes. Bijdrage tot de kennis van de opvoeding hier te lande in de achttiende eeuw* (Rotterdam: Brusse, 1908); P.L. van Eck, "Van Alphen als kinderdichter," *Groot-Nederland* (1908), 213–38.
[56] We refer to the following editions: Christian Felix Weisse, *Lieder und Fabeln für Kinder und junge Leute. Nach des Verfassers Wunsche gesammelt und herausgegeben von M. Samuel Gottlob Frisch* (Leipzig, 1807); Gottlob Wilhelm Burmann, *Kleine Lieder für Mädchen, und Jünglinge* (Berlin, 1777).
[57] "My dog is a good animal;/The moment I call, it follows me." Weisse, "Der Gehorsam" (Obedience), in *Lieder*, 13.
[58] "Pious, pious I will be on earth,/And already as a boy/I will enjoy being near God;/Grown up by Religion" Burmann, "Frommigkeit," in *Kleine Lieder*, 74.

forward in poems such as Weisse's "Der Schatten" [The Shadow], in which a child wishes to be as big as his shadow, and "An die Spinne" [To the Spider], in which a child first admires the spider for its ability to weave such an ingenious web; when he sees it catching a fly, his admiration turns into dismay. Nevertheless, most of the poems deal exclusively with virtues, often voiced by a child, like Burmann's "Der Gehorsam" [Obedience]:

> Ich solte nicht gehorsam seyn?
> Nicht meine Eltern Stimme hören?
> O dann würd ich mein Herz entehren,
> Und würde Ihre Huld entweyhn!
>
> Ich bin ein Kind, ich weiß noch nicht
> Mich selbst zu bilden, selbst zu bessern;
> Gehorsam soll mein Herz vergrössern
> Und Freude sey mir diese Pflicht!
>
> Nein, guter Himmel! Laß mich nie
> Durch Ungehorsam heßlich werden;
> Und meiner Eltern Luft auf Erden
> Sey ich durch Folgsamkeit schon früh![59]

The lyrical subject (I) is a boy. But the boy is wise enough to realise that he is not wise enough to educate himself. Therefore, he proclaims the importance of obedience to his parents and states that he acts upon this virtue happily. Although Burmann seems to present an individual child by using a first-person narrator, the lyrical I stands for the child in general. It represents an ideal (male) child. It voices the virtue which the implied author (the discursive presence of Burmann in the poem) wants to transmit.

Inspired by Burmann and Weisse, Van Alphen also incorporated children's perspectives into his poems. In his time, Dutch children did not lack reading material, as we have seen, but the previous children's literature did not pay much attention to the child's point of view. The first-person narrators of Burmann and Weisse, together with the increased interest in the child's character prompted by the Enlightened interest in education, inspired van Alphen to combine his knowledge of, and experience with, real children with Enlightenment educational ambitions and the ideal of the perfect child.

He situated many of his poems more explicitly in the living environment of children than did his predecessors, and his poems dealt more directly with the children's feelings and experiences. Wirth, who was later to consider children's literature prior to that by van Alphen as "improper children's literature", wrote:

> Then there was van Alphen with stories about tops, hoops, puppies, plums, peaches, waffles and other subjects that occupied the minds of children, though not on a daily

---

[59]'Obedience/Would I not be obedient?/Not hear my parents' voices?/It would be to my heart's disgrace,/and I would not get their praise!/I am a child, I do not know yet/how to educate myself, how to improve myself;/Obedience will grow my heart/And this duty will bring me joy!/No, for heaven's sake! Do not let/me become disagreeable;/And I will be my parents' joy/by being obedient early on." Burmann, *Kleine Lieder*, 33.

basis: thunderstorms, dying, friendship, pity, religion, etc. (…) We may safely assume these were the first poems in which the child felt they belonged to its domain (…).[60]

Not only did van Alphen situate his poems in the world of children, but he also – as did Weisse and Burmann – gave them a voice with which they could articulate their feelings and thoughts about their world, either literally by incorporating a child as the first-person narrator of the poem or by using a third-person narrator looking through the child's eyes, often using free indirect speech, ("Erlebte Rede"). However, whereas Weisse and Burmann's child narrators and subjects of focus are merely vocalisers, the adult being the implied author (i.e. *the master's voice*), Van Alphen put forward much more childlike protagonists who tried to use the child's voice. A comparison of "Schule" [School] by Burmann and "The Swallows" by van Alphen will illustrate this:

Schule

O wie ists so schön:
In die Schule zo gehn,
Und zu lernen darinn!
Jeder Augenblick
Wird fürs herz ein Glück,
Wird der Seele gewinn!

Meines Lehrers Schweiß,
Meinen rühmlichen Fleiß
Sieht der gütige Gott!
Und er legt darein
Segen und Gedeyhn,
Dieser zärtliche Gott!

Früher himmelwärts
Schwing ich Knabe mein Herz,
Wenn ich Tugend erlernt!
Engel lieben mich,
Wenn früh von mir sich
Jede Unart entfernt.

The swallows
A story

Kees was going to school for the first time,
But right after stepping down the pavement,
He seemed to feel dissatisfied:
He stood wondering, his head up.
He saw the swallows floating to and fro,
And said, that is living for joy.
A man at the street,
Heard little Kees,
Laughing, he pulled him aside;
And said: Don't you know they have to
They are catching flies to feed their young,
That otherwise would be hungry.
You just call this joy, no little Kees! you're wrong.
But you know what you can learn from it?
Their cheerful floating
Can be an example for you,
About how to do ones duty industriously and joyfully;
And how ugly it looks, if one has to be forced.
* * *
I will go to school, Kees said: that is a good lesson![61]

---

[60]"Toen kwam Van Alphen met verhalen van tollen, hoepels, jonge honden, pruimen, perziken, wafels en daarnaast ook onderwerpen, die 't kind ook wel degelik konden bezig houden, al was dit niet zo dageliks: onweer, sterven, vriendschap, medelijden, godsdienst, enz. … We kunnen gerust aannemen, dat dit de eerste gedichtjes zijn geweest waarin 't kind voelde, dat men in zijn sfeer kwam …', L.J.Th. Wirth, *Een eeuw kinderpoëzie 1778–1878* (Groningen: J.B. Wolters, 1926), 48–9.
[61]"De zwaluwen/Eene vertelling/Kees zou voor 't eerst naar school toe gaan,/Maar was de stoep pas afgetreden,/Of't scheen, hij was niet wel te vreden;/En bleef, het hoofd om hoog, een poos verwonderd staan./Hij zag de zwaluwen zo heen en weder zweeven,/En zei, dat heet eerst regt op zijn vermaak te leven./Een man die zig op straat bevond,/En Keesjes meening ras verstond,/Trok hem, al lagchend, wat ter zijden;/En zei: wel weetge niet, dat zij dit moeten doen,/Zij vangen vliegjes, om hun jongen mee te voen,/Die anders honger moesten lijden./Noemt gij dit slegts vermaak, neen Keesje! dat is mis,/Maar weet gij wat hier uit voor u te leeren is?/Zij kunnen, door dit lustig zweven,/Aan u een voorbeeld geven,/En dat het lelijk staat, als men 't gedwongen doet./Hoe men met vlijt en vreugd zijn werk verrigten moet/***/Ik loop naar school, zei Kees: die les is zeker goed!" (Van Alphen, *Kleine Gedigten*, 151).

MODES AND MEANING: DISPLAYS OF EVIDENCE IN EDUCATION

Die Religion
Hört mich lallenden Sohn
Aus dem Himmel schon an!
Gegnet mein Bemühn,
Läßt mich Laster fliehn,

Führt mich ebene Bahn.
Früh hat jeder Trieb
Alle Tugenden lieb,
Meine Seele wird gut;

Jede Wissenschaft,
Macht mich tugendhaft,
Schenkt zur Weisheit mir Muth.

O der Schule sey
Stets mein Wille getreu,
Stets sey lernen mir Luft!
Weisheit kan erhöhn!
Gern zur Schule gehn:
Sey mein Adel der Brust.[62]

Both poems deal with a child going to school and propound the importance of going to school. Burmann's poem has a first-person narrator: a child. This child praises the school for its impartation of knowledge and virtues. It even voices the slogan of the Enlightenment literally, stating "Jede Wissenschaft,/Macht mir tugendhaft". The child does not have the least objection to going to school and expects God to see him going and love him for it. The poem depicts only a given moment in time and shows no development; it is an ode to school from the beginning to the end.

Van Alphen's poem presents a boy, Kees, who goes to school for the first time. Note that the child in this poem has been given a name and a sex and is thereby more of an individual than the first-person narrator in Burmann's poem, which seems to represent the child in general, although implicitly assuming that the child is a boy. Whereas Burmann's child states that going to school is the best thing, Kees does not feel like going at all. He'd rather fly around freely, like the swallows he spots in the air. However, a passer-by overhears him. This man, obviously the spokesman for the implied author, cleverly uses Kees' own observation and turns it

---

[62] 'School/Oh how good it is:/To go to school,/And to learn!/Every moment/Is a heart's joy,/ and a soul's profit!/My tutor's sweat,/My honourable diligence/Is seen by the good Lord!/ And He gives/His blessing and approval,/ This loving God!/I send to heaven/My heart,/When I learn the virtues!/The angels love me,/When early on/Vices stay far from me./Religion/Is heard by me, stammering son/From heaven!/Gains my interest,/Sends away my vices,/Keeps me to the straight path./Early on every lad/Gets to love the virtues,/My soul gets well;/ Knowledge,/Makes me virtuous,/Gives wisdom to my heart./Oh school is/What I want,/To learn is my heart's desire!/Wisdom is able to uplift!/Happily going to school:/Is my proud and joy." Burmann, *Kleine Lieder*, 76–8.

into an allegory. He points out how the swallows are not free at all, but do their duty – that is, their cheerful flying serves to catch flies to feed their young. Instantly, Kees realises he should perform his duty diligently and joyfully as well, and so goes on to school.

Van Alphen put forward the same moral message as Burmann: a child is obliged to go to school and to be happy about it. However, instead of presenting a child voicing this moral without counterforces, he presents a child who has to deal with an opposing desire, the desire to be free. Contrary to Burmann's child, van Alphen's child, Kees, does not know right from wrong at the beginning, but changes his mind about going to school during the poem. Through the allegory of the swallows, his desire to have fun is replaced by the realisation that everyone has to perform his duty and his is going to school. Consequently, the poem presents the development of Kees from an ignorant child to a child taking his first steps to becoming an Enlightened adult. Moreover, van Alphen represents the Enlightenment faith in the child's rationality.[63] The man's moral reasoning immediately takes root in Kees. Whereas Burmann presents a child who is merely a vocaliser of the implied adult author from the beginning, an ideal child, van Alphen makes room for the notion of development and growing up which characterises real children.

This does not mean that Kees is not an ideal child as well, for he ends up voicing the same moral as Burmann's child narrator. However, unlike Burmann, van Alphen makes space for a more childlike perspective, which child readers should have been able to recognise. His poem accounts for the process of development, the process of growing up and learning before internalising an ideal. Thus, his poems not only seem to incorporate a child's perspective while just using the child as a vocaliser, but actually take account of the nature of the child. Inspired by the use by Weisse and Burmann of the child to provide focus, van Alphen took the incorporation of the child's perspective a step further by not only displaying the ideal result of moral education but also representing the process.

Family first

A striking difference between the poems of van Alphen and his German sources of inspiration is the setting of the poems: no concrete setting is given in most of Burmann's and Weisse's poems, but van Alphen situates his verses predominantly within the immediate family circle. Father, mother, brothers and sisters pass in review, as occasionally, as the poems are situated in a bourgeois milieu, does someone in the service of the family, such as a gardener or a nurse.

Conversely, Burmann only mentions a father or a mother occasionally: in fewer than seven of the 75 poems of the 1777 edition. And even when mentioned, they do not play a direct role in the poems. Next to father and mother, Weisse presents siblings as well, but a setting in the family circle occurs in less than nine of his 148 poems in the 1807 edition. Van Alphen, by contrast, situates 25 of his 66 poems directly within the family circle if we take only the text into account. If we consider the illustrations Jacob Buijs made under van Alphen's direct supervision[64] as well, only 10 poems are *not* situated within the family.

---

[63] Cf. Wolff, *Proeve*.
[64] Buijnsters, "Nawoord," 188.

Van Alphen wrote his poems in a typically Dutch Enlightened vein. The family home as the predominant environment for moral education formed the core of Dutch Enlightened bourgeois ideology.[65] Enlightenment-inspired writers such as van Alphen combined the interests of the state and the family in their longing for citizenship for all and so emphasised the role of family education in the formation of virtuous future citizens. Education in the family would eventually serve to strengthen the state.

The many learned societies that were established from the 1750s on, such as the *Dutch Society of Sciences* founded in 1752 in the city of Haarlem and the above-mentioned *Society for the Common Good*, organised hundreds of contests on ideas how to deal with societal issues, many on education and the family, to encourage citizens to contribute to the national debate.[66] The mainstream Dutch Enlightenment writers, while also aiming at making primary education compulsory, considered the family to be the primary educational institution, which therefore, should be supported by the state through regulations and encouragement. They emphasised preparation for citizenship as the new and primary goal of family education. Consequently, writers such as van Alphen with his child-oriented poems, Martinet with his *Domestic Book for Dutch Families* (*Huisboek voor vaderlandsche huisgezinnen*, 1793), Justus van Effen with his plea for the education of girls (1731) – in function of their future duties as wives and mothers[67] – and many other authors of texts on education, such as those published in the news magazine *Dutch Spectator* (*Hollandsche Spectator*) – including female writers of pamphlets and books for both adults and adolescents such as Betje Wolff and Aagje Deken – and children's writers – such as Petronella Moens – continued centuries of the Dutch tradition of praising the superiority of the family in the realm of education, now with a new goal: raising new citizens for the not yet existing but already dreamt of unified nation.[68]

In his focus on family education, to be interpreted as education in service of the nation state, Van Alphen also differed in another way from his German examples. Not only did Weisse and Burmann situate much fewer poems within the family circle, but they also practised another way of spreading patriotism. Burmann, especially, wrote much more explicit poems on patriotism, such as "Vaterlandsliebe" [Patriotism], "Die Würde der Ordnung" [The Value of Order], "Rühne Gedanken eines Knaben" [Quiet Thoughts of a Boy] and "Tägliche Gedanken ein Deutschen kleinen Jünglings" [Daily Thoughts of a Little German Boy].[69] This suited the German dream of national unity, which was politically still a long time coming but was already being culturally experienced as such.[70] Van Alphen, on the other hand, wrote only one poem explicitly on patriotism (discussed above), and adopted the Dutch Enlightened strategy of family education in the service of moulding children

---

[65]Dekker, *Het verlangen*, 198.
[66]Wijnandus Wilhelmus Mijnhardt, *Tot Heil van 't menschdom. Culturele genootschappen in Nederland 1750–1815* (Amsterdam: Rodopi, 1987).
[67]Justus van Effen, *Hollandsche Spectator* 17 (1731), quoted by Kloek & Mijnhardt, *1800*, 249.
[68]Kloek and Mijnhardt, *1800*, 250–2; Dorothée Sturkenboom, *Spectators van de hartstocht. Sekse en emotionele cultuur in de achttiende eeuw* (Hilversum: Verloren, 1998).
[69]Burmann, *Kleine Lieder*, 105, 107, 109, 144.
[70]Cf. T. Nipperdey, *Deutsche Geschichte 1800–1866. Bürgerwelt und starker Staat* (München: Beck, 1983).

into good citizens for the nation. Within the family circle, children would acquire the typical Dutch Enlightened definition of contentment as the best kind of happiness. There they would learn to practise virtue, control desires and impulses and balance head and heart.[71]

The children in the poems by van Alphen learn all virtues belonging to the Enlightened norm pattern from either their parents or their siblings. Father and mother pass them on by example, while siblings function as mirroring images or reproving counterparts to collide with or practice their virtues on. For example, Alexis, in the poem "Alexis", practises love for one's fellow man in relation to his sister but has not yet succeeded in making this love unconditional; he loves his sister when she does what he wants but stops loving her when she does not. This brings the authoritarian narrator to the rhetorical question: "A love, so quickly cooling down,/Solely aiming at one's own crown,/Could that be real love?"[72] In the poem "Klaartje and Keetje", little Keet reprimands her sister Klaartje when the latter prefers playing over learning her lessons: "Never working, never reading,/always being in the garden,/Is it that one lives for?/Dear Klaartje, stop playing;/Oh! it must bore you, all this time/you devote to your dolls."[73] In "Klaasje and Pietje", little Piet teaches Klaasje the Enlightened aversion to fantasy figures and mocks the method of educating children by threatening with a bogyman: "Whoever believes of such a kind,/Has been robbed of his mind".[74] In "The fighting boys", little Gijs and little Klaas dispute about the best way to settle their argument – by fighting or by fatherly mediation.[75] Even the family dog may function as a stumbling block: in one of van Alphen's posthumous poems, "The Feasting Dog", little Piet is reprimanded for his jealousy of the attention his father gives to his dog. "It's envy, Piet!", Piet's father exclaims, "because this animal/Has sometimes given me joy./Is that the reason you can't stand it?/ Did I ever love the animal/like I love you? ... Pooh! Jealous boy!" Crying, little Piet slinks off.[76]

The role of nature

The theme of nature and childhood is just the opposite of family education. It occurs occasionally in Van Alphen's poems, while his German predecessors, especially Weisse, were quite fond of it. In most of Van Alphen's poems concerning nature, it functions as an allegory, as a moral mirror of human behaviour. For example, in the poem "The Wilted Rose" (De verwelkte roos), in which little Jan asks why a rose wilts so quickly and then is reprimanded by his father for carping at God's creation, he is told: "The Creator best of all knows,/Why it has to wilt so quickly;/He wants

---

[71] Ellen Jacoba Krol, *De smaak der natie. Opvattingen over huiselijkheid in de Noord-Nederlandse poëzie van 1800–1840* (Hilversum: Verloren, 1997), 23–52, 56–9.
[72] "Een liefde, die zo ras verkoelt,/Die slegts op eigen voordeel doelt,/Zou dat wel regte liefde wezen?" Van Alphen, *Kleine Gedigten*, 21.
[73] "Nooit te werken, nooit te lezen,/Altoos in den tuin te weezen,/Is het daarom dat men left?/ Klaartje lief, hou op met spelen;/Ach! de tijd moet u verveelen,/Dien gij aan uw poppen geeft." Van Alphen, *Kleine Gedigten*, 73.
[74] "Die aan zulk een man gelooft,/Is van zijn verstand beroofd." Van Alphen, *Kleine Gedigten*, 83.
[75] Van Alphen, *Kleine Gedigten*, 131.
[76] Van Alphen, *Kleine Gedigten*, 169–71.
[77] "De Schepper weet het best van allen,/Waarom 't zo schielijk af moet vallen;/En wil ook, datge gadeslaat,/Hoe ras het aardsche schoon vergaat." Van Alphen, *Kleine Gedigten*, 139.

you to see,/How quickly the earth's beauty goes".[77] Many poems, such as "Devoutness" (De godsdienstigheid) and "Winter's Song" (Winterzang), present nature as proof of God's goodness and wisdom. A few poems, however, go beyond allegory and seeking to provide proof of God's wisdom and represent the awakening of a more sensitive and sentimental Enlightenment mentality and the first signs of the transition to Romanticism in the late eighteenth century. In "Little Singer-girl", little Chris evokes a sensitive mood picture by night:[78]

> The twinkling stars
> brighten the dark;
> The glowing moon
> Has begun to spread
> Her glance over the meadows,
> And plays with the leaves.[79]

While the surroundings of the family and the family home are the main setting in van Alphen's poems for children, nature predominates in those of Weisse. In many poems by both Burmann and Weisse, nature functions as an allegory for human behaviour or as a reason to praise God's creation. Weisse was particularly fond of natural allegories, which can be seen in the titles of his poems alone: "Das Veilchen" [The Violet], "An einem Baum im Herbste" [At an Autumn Tree], "Die Bienen" [The Bees], "An einen Bach" [At a Brook], "Auf einen durch eine Sturm niedergestürtste Linde" [About a Fallen Linden Tree].[80] In these poems the lyrical I, almost always representing the child, learns from the course of nature, either in relation to animals or growth. The opening poem is especially notable. "Der junge Baum" [The Young Tree] not only presents a pedagogical allegory but refers to the simile of the child as a young tree which was very popular in the eighteenth century:

> Das liebe kleine Bäumchen hier
> Ist, wie man sagt, gleich alt wie mir,
> Und trägt, so jung und zart,
> Schon Früchten von den besten Art.
>
> Es lohnt dem Gärtner, dessen Hand
> So vielen Fleiß darauf verwandt:
> Wie wird es ihn erfreun,
> Wird es zum Baum erwachsen seyn!
>
> O! Bin ich nicht dem Bäumchen gleich?

---

[77]"De Schepper weet het best van allen,/Waarom 't zo schielijk af moet vallen;/En wil ook, datge gadeslaat,/Hoe ras het aardsche schoon vergaat." Van Alphen, *Kleine Gedigten*, 139.
[78]Buijnsters, "Nawoord," 186.
[79]"Het starrengeflonker/Vervrolijkt het donker;/De lichtende maan/Begint op de weiden/Haar glansen te spreiden/En speelt door de blaên." Van Alphen, *Kleine Gedigten*, 124.
[80]Weisse, *Lieder*, 26, 31, 93, 95, 103.

Zwar jetzt nur noch am Blüten reich:
Doch giebt mir Gott gedeihn;
So will ichs auch an Früchten seyn.[81]

The young lyrical subject of this poem admires the fruit a young tree bears and realises how much joy this will give the gardener who raised it. He or she extrapolates this to him/herself and expresses the wish to become as full of fruit as well – with fruit obviously metaphorically referring to virtues. At the same time this poem refers to the popular pedagogical simile of the balance between letting a child grow freely and constant pruning and guiding. Enlightenment pedagogues argued that children should be able to grow up freely, like young trees – but needing, however, some steering by adults to grow in the right direction, just as a tree needs steering by occasional trimming and binding.[82]

Moreover, the lyrical subject, the child, realises that it needs God to "blossom" like the tree. God is a natural presence in many of Weisse's poems, as also in Burmann's. The child narrators often directly invoke Him or refer to Him as an almighty presence and providence. However, there are no signs of a particular religious denomination. The same holds for van Alphen's children's poems.

Religion

Van Alphen was a practicing Protestant Christian. In his early twenties he had converted to pietism, and for the rest of his life he would call this conversion his rebirth.[83] A few years later, the urge of a personal testimony drove him to start writing devotional poetry. Together with his friend Pieter Leonard van de Kasteele, he published four volumes in which they versified the way to salvation and the service of God.[84] Conversely, when van Alphen started writing poetry for children, he omitted every explicit reference to religious dogmas such as original sin, redemption, heaven and hell.[85] God is highly present in many poems, but rewards and punishments are restricted to life on earth and not projected on the hereafter. Moreover, God is referred to only as a loving father. Thus the first lines of the poem "The Happiness of Infancy" (Het kinderlijk geluk) read:

I am a child,
Loved by God,
And born for good fortune.

---

[81] "The young tree/This sweet small tree here/Is, as they say, as old as I am,/And bears, so young and fresh,/Already the best of fruits./It was worth the gardener's/Hard work:/How happy he will be,/When the tree will be fully grown!/Oh! Am I not like the little tree?/Still full of blossoms:/But if God lets me flourish;/I will bear fruits as well." Weisse, Lieder und Fabeln, 3.
[82] Cf. A. Baggerman and R. Dekker, "Het spook van Sion. Veranderende visies op jeugd en natuur in de late achttiende eeuw," *De achttiende eeuw* 36 (2004): 143–56, 159–60.
[83] Buijnsters, *Hieronymus*, 34.
[84] *Proeve van Stichtelijke Mengel-Poëzij* (1771), *Stigtelijke Mengelpoëzij. Eerste Stukjen* (1772), *Stigtelijke Mengelpoëzij. Tweede Stukjen* (1773) and *Stigtelijke Mengelpoëzij. Derde Stukjen* (1782).
[85] Buijnsters, "Nawoord,' 185.

His love is great;
I've got toys, clothes, milk and bread,
A cradle to sleep in.[86]

However, some years after van Alphen finished his last volume of children's poetry, he wrote another work for his children, in which religion, religious doctrines and profession of faith were the main themes: *Gronden mijner geloofs-belijdenis, opengelegd voor mijne kinderen* [Grounds of My Profession of Faith, Disclosed for My Children]. His sons were 13, 14 and 15 years old at the time, and van Alphen wanted to prepare them for their confirmation. His motives for writing the book correspond to his motives for writing his children's poems some years before: the available religious instruction books were beyond a child's comprehension. Now van Alphen wanted to attune his catechesis to the young. In this book, van Alphen does show his religious preferences and expounds his Reformed denomination.[87]

The reason van Alphen waited until his children were older once again shows his awareness of the process of a child's development, due to which he waited for his children to be old enough to become acquainted with the specificities of Calvinism. The final lines of the opening poem of van Alphen's third volume of children's poems indicate this explicitly. They read: "You will get greater books,/when you have grown some more."[88] Van Alphen thought children up to the age of 10 too young to be bombarded with dogmatic arguments. Following Weisse and Burmann, he adhered to the Philanthropinist approach of a broadly confessional education. The children in his poems sing the praises of God and Jesus, strive for virtuousness in the eyes of God and ask Him for forgiveness when they have done wrong, but one does not see them going to church or confirmation class. The absence of denominational doctrines is another reason accounting for the popularity of the poems: they were suitable for children of all denominations – although the lack of dogmatic instruction also met with some objections by orthodox believers.[89] In reserving religious dogmas for older children, van Alphen, following the example of the Philanthropinists, once again acknowledged a phased development of children.

Conclusion

Hieronijmus van Alphen successfully adopted and adapted existing educational strategies, such as the moral poetics developed by his German predecessors Christian Felix Weisse and Gottlob Wilhelm Burmann. Taking Weisse's and Burmann's strategies on a poetic journey from Germany to the Netherlands, he not only transferred them but also transformed them, and he did so in a specifically Dutch Enlightened utilitarian way. His poems could be read for fun – both by children and by their parents – but ultimately they were intended to instruct. In line with the Dutch

---

[86]"Ik ben een kind,/Van God bemind,/En tot geluk geschapen./Zijn liefde is groot;/'k Heb speelgoed, kleedren, melk en brood,/ Een wieg om in te slapen" (Van Alphen, *Kleine Gedigten*, 15).
[87]Buijnsters, *Hieronymus*, 218–22.
[88]"Grooter boeken zult ge krijgen,/Als gij ook wat grooter zijt" (Van Alphen, *Kleine Gedichten*, 117).
[89]For example, the line "tot geluk geschapen" [born for luck] conflicted with the Calvinistic doctrine of predestination. Clarisse, "Over Hieronijmus van Alphen, als dichter en kinderdichter. Twee voorlezingen," *De Fakkel* (1831–1831).

Enlightened educational culture of the late eighteenth century, his poems were useful and entertaining at the same time. This was possible because he took the life and living environment of children into account and took particular account of the concept of development as a distinguishing characteristic of the specific nature of the child with which child readers could identify.

Van Alphen adopted a series of specific topics of Weisse and Burmann, making use of the catalogue of subjects that they had already developed in their poems and using the child's voice, with the child as the lyrical subject. Apart from adopting those elements, van Alphen also substantially transformed the poetics he was inspired by. He developed a more child-oriented style by taking into consideration the specific moral development of the child, which made him a moral development psychologist *avant la lettre*. Furthermore, by situating almost all of the poems in a family context – this also in contrast with the poems by Weisse and Burmann – he made clear that with regard to educating children, it was family first. But the poems were also read at school, and he even recommended that teachers read them in class. The poems, described as the "laudable Enlightenment Pedagogics by Hieronijmus van Alphen", received a central place on the *General List of Books for Primary Schools in the Northern Provinces of the Kingdom of the Netherlands* in 1815, drawn up with the educational ambition of determining what Dutch primary school children should read and what they should not. It was a typically Enlightenment-based list drawn up by the influential philanthropic society, *The Society for the Common Good*, which was founded in 1784. The list advised schoolteachers what stories should be read by their pupils, omitting everything supernatural, such as fantastic reading material or tales about Catholic saints, while recommending useful reading material, such as van Alphen's poems.[90] Van Alphen's poems also continued to be read at school both in the Netherlands and in Flanders even after the Second World War, as we have already illustrated with the example of Lodewick's popular textbook on the history of Dutch literature. Until well into the 1960s, poems like "The Plum Tree" were learned by heart by pupils in schools, and even nowadays, the poems by van Alphen have not entirely disappeared from the school curriculum. In a document from *Stichting Poetry International & Stichting Lezen Vlaanderen*, published for the eleventh Poetry Day on 28 November 2010 and intended to help primary school teachers encourage their pupils to read poems, Van Alphen was not absent; a rap version of his famous poem "The Plum Tree" was brought to the readers' attention – a transformation Van Alphen could never have dreamt of. His poems were also listed in the document's bibliography, albeit with reference not to his own publications but to anthologies of Dutch poems. The reason for this is very clear from the document in question: Van Alphen's emphasis on moral development and on learning the virtues is no longer part of present-day children's worlds. Poems promoting goodness and decency as ideal child behaviour can remain part of the collective memory albeit only through irony and rap, it seems from this 2010 document. And yet Van Alphen, while not inventing reading material for children, did succeed in creating reading material that satisfied Enlightened pedagogical ideas on

---

[90] P.J. Buijnsters and Leontine Buijnsters-Smets, *Lust en leering*, 46–47; P.J. Buijnsters, "Het eeuwenoude storiegoed," in *De mondige jeugdliteratuur*, ed. Piet Mooren, Jeanne Kurvers, and Helma van Lierop-Debrauwer (Leidschendam: Biblion Uitgeverij, 2004), 39–40; cf. J.J.H. Dekker, *Educational Ambitions in History. Childhood and Education in an Expanding Educational Space from the Seventeenth to the Twentieth Century* (Frankfurt am Main: Peter Lang, 2010), 78–9.

fostering virtue while acknowledging the voice and the distinct feature of the concept of development of its young addressees. In writing for children and trying to put himself both in the position of the child and of the parent, Van Alphen was an innovator in the Dutch educational culture of the late eighteenth century.[91] He expanded the educational space[92] by scaling down the point of view in reading material for children. As a result, Van Alphen's poems became part of the collective Dutch and Flemish memory, which inevitably went together with re-inventions and disruptions of the meanings originally associated with them.

---

[91]Sturkenboom, *Spectators*; Jonathan Israel, *The Dutch Republic, Its Rise, Greatness, and Fall 1477–1806* (Clarendon Press: Oxford, 1995), 1062.
[92]Cf. Dekker, *Educational Ambitions in History*, 11–15.

Moving frontiers of empire: production, travel and transformation through technologies of display

Natasha Macnab, Ian Grosvenor and Kevin Myers

School of Education, University of Birmingham, England

Introduction

Over the past two decades there has been a growing interest in the exploration of "transnational history". This work has focused in general on understanding the "movement, ebb and circulation" of ideas across borders and in particular on the introduction, transmission, reception and appropriation of ideas through the process of cultural transfer.[1] This interest in the transnational and cultural transfer at the same time has been paralleled by an increasing use of spatialised approaches to understand the making and maintenance of knowledge and the influence in particular of geographies of texts, talk and testimony.[2] Historians in recent years, whether operating within a "transnational" or a "spatial" paradigm, have given increasing attention to the role of exhibitions in the circulation of ideas and practices and to the power of the visual in carrying knowledge across borders.[3]

This article is an attempt to engage with methodological questions associated with adopting a transnational or spatial approach by exploring two case studies involving texts, travel and translation. The first case study, from the late nineteenth century to the period up to the Second World War, considers the transmission role of annual reports of a charitable institution dedicated to projects of social reform which linked England, Canada and Australia. In particular, attention will be focused on the construction, function and reception of photographic evidence "displayed" in the reports.

---

[1]Gabriela Ossenbach and Maria Del Mar del Pozo, "Postcolonial Models, Cultural Transfers and Transnational Perspectives in Latin America: A Research Agenda," *Paedagogica Historica* 47, no. 5 (2011): 579–600; Martin Lawn, ed., *An Atlantic Crossing? The Work of the International Examination Inquiry, its Researchers, Methods and Influence* (Oxford: Symposium, 2008).
[2]David Livingstone, *Putting Science in its Place: Geographies of Scientific Knowledge* (Chicago: CUP, 2003); David Livingstone, "Text, Talk and Testimony: Geographical Reflections on Scientific Habits. An Afterword," *British Journal for the History of Science* 38, no. 136 (2005): 93–100; P.K. Gilbert, *Mapping the Victorian Social Body* (Albany, NY: Suny, 2004); I. Grosvenor, "Geographies of Risk: An Exploration of City Childhoods in Early Twentieth Century Britain,' *Paedagogica Historica* 45, 1&2 (2009): 215–34.
[3]Joost Coté, "'To See is to Know": The Pedagogy of the Colonial Exhibition, Semarang, 1914," *Paedagogica Historica* 36, no. 1 (2000): 340–66; Elizabeth Edwards, *Raw Histories: Photographs, Anthropology and Museums* (Oxford: Berg, 2001).

The second case study is from the latter half of the twentieth century and analyses campaigns for textbook revisions that drew inspiration and resources from people and ideas that journeyed across national boundaries. The analysis here focuses on the formation of communities of interpretation whose coming together enabled the production of new kinds of ideas and their representation in new educational spaces and technologies.

In choosing what appear to be thematically distinct topics from different periods, the article is concerned with the publication of different kinds of educational texts – some directly didactic, others more informally so; it considers mechanisms for travel in two different periods and explores the ways in which "reliable knowledge" travels.[4] This knowledge was united by its concern for and engagement with what Bill Schwarz has called "the frontiers of empire".[5] These frontiers might have been spatial, pictorial, textual or imaginative, but all attempted to impose order, to unify and homogenise otherwise chaotic populations and groups.

Philanthropic child migration was reported as the extension of civilization, "the conquering of nature and natives", in colonial Canada and Australia and, as the first case study shows, a certain version of those events entered the imaginations, the very structures of feeling, in metropolitan Britain.[6] Those distinctively imperial structures of feeling may have been affected by decolonisation and the end of Empire but, as the second case study demonstrates, their psychic force and the constitutive role they played in the national imagination did not disappear.[7] Imperial authority, enacted in child migration schemes and displayed in annual reports, helped to silence histories of migration to England and to associate black people with conquered natives. However, they were also open to contestation.[8] In the ascription of meaning to images, in the collective and critical reading of texts and in the campaigns that enabled new knowledge travel to public spaces, new voices began to translate existing stories of empire.

Case 1: The Children's Emigration Homes
Context

The late nineteenth century in Northern Europe and North America was a period of accelerated processes of modernisation, which demanded rapid accommodation to new conditions. Economic and industrial developments increasingly involved the state in planning and managing change. In particular, there were concerns and

---

[4] Peter Howlett and Mary S. Morgan, eds., *How Well do Facts Travel? The Dissemination of Reliable Knowledge* (Cambridge: CUP, 2011). We would like to thank Frank Simon for bringing this volume to our attention.
[5] Bill Schwarz, *The White Man's World: Memories of Empire Volume I* (Oxford: Oxford University Press, 2011), 1–13.
[6] Schwarz, *White Man's World*, 12. More generally see Catherine Hall, *Civilising Subjects: Metropole and Colony in the English Imagination, 1830–1867* (Cambridge: Polity, 2002); Sonya O. Rose, *Which People's War? National Identity and Citizenship in Wartime Britain, 1939–1945* (Oxford: Oxford University Press, 2003).
[7] Schwarz, *White Man's World*, 33–52. For some of the formal educational mechanisms supporting these structures of feeling see Ian Grosvenor, "'There's no place like home': Education and the Making of National Identity," *History of Education* 28, no. 3 (1999): 235–50.
[8] For examples of silenced memories and particularly pertinent discussions of domestic racism see Lucy Bland, "White Women and Men of Colour: Miscegenation Fears in Britain after the Great War," *Gender and History* 17, no. 1 (2005): 29–61; Jacqueline Jenkinson, *Black 1919: Riots, Racism and Resistance in Imperial Britain* (Liverpool: Liverpool University Press, 2009).

pessimistic preoccupations with the threats to social and political stability posed by the unemployable "residuum" and their progeny who were drawn to city environs. Cities, consequently, gradually became involved in the systematisation of knowledge, in the compiling, checking and synthesising of information about their populations – their rates of fertility, their susceptibility to disease, their physical attributes, their mental capacities and their morals. Data were collected on populations that had previously constituted an opaque mass and new categories of people emerged – categories which had material consequences for individuals so counted and classified. One of the important technological advancements which enabled the population and their condition to be known in this period of dramatic change was the rise of photography. The emergence of this new "objective" medium offered the state a way to survey and fix the external world and to closely scrutinise it for evidence.[9] Once the governed were identifiable and knowable, they could be operated upon to secure governance.[10] "Knowing" the population and acting upon that knowledge was also an agenda for philanthropic bodies, particularly those associated with addressing a perceived urban childcare crisis.[11] Amongst these bodies were the Children's Emigration Homes.

The Children's Emigration Homes (CEH) were established in 1872 by John T. Middlemore who bought a house for boys in September 1872, on St. Luke's Road, Birmingham, England, and subsequently purchased a home for girls on nearby Spring Street. The objective of the homes was "to rescue boys and girls from lives of crime and destitution". The method in which this was achieved was by removing any children "likely to become criminals and paupers, from the homes and surroundings which seem certain to prove fatal to them, and transferring them by means of emigration to different and hopeful associations".[12]

If the children were considered physically and mentally fit for emigration, then they would be received into the homes in Birmingham, trained there for a year and subsequently taken to Canada. Children were taken not because "*they* are wicked, but because their associations will make them so. We take them to lead them out of temptation... the true Arab child is very lovable"[13] (in the late Victorian period, an underclass of children known as street Arabs became commonplace in the discourse around children of the street, and their very name evoked frightening outsider status).[14] By 1925, due to the Bondfield Report a year earlier, which stated that

---

[9] John Tagg, *The Burden of Representation* (Houndmills: Macmillan, 1988), 66–102.
[10] See Ian Grosvenor and Kevin Myers, "Progressivism, Control and Correction: Local Education Authorities and Educational Policy in 20th Century England," *Paedagogica Historica* 42, nos. 1&2 (2006): 225–48.
[11] See Xiaobei Chen, *Tending the Gardens of Citizenship. Child Saving in Toronto 1880s-1920s* (Toronto: Toronto University Press, 2005); Roy Parker, *Uprooted. The Shipment of Poor Children to Canada, 1867–1917* (Bristol: Policy Press, 2008); Robert Kershaw and Janet Sacks, *New Lives for Old. The Story of Britain's Child Migrants* (London: The National Archives, 2008); Shirlee Swain and Margot Hillel, *Child, Nation, Race and Empire. Child Rescue Discourse, England, Canada and Australia, 1850–1915* (Manchester: Manchester University Press, 2010); Jessie B. Ramey, *Childcare in Black and White. Working Parents and the History of Orphanages* (Urbana: University of Illinois Press, 2012).
[12] Children's Emigration Homes [CEH], *Nineteenth Annual Report* (Birmingham, 1891).
[13] CEH, *Fourth Annual Report* (Birmingham, 1876) 5. Italics in the original.
[14] Anna Davin, "Waif Stories in Late Nineteenth Century England", *History Workshop Journal*, 52 (2001): 68. See for example the work of the journalist James Greenwood in *The True History of a Little Ragamuffin* (1868) and Charles Dickens, *Bleak House* (1853). See also Nancy Rose Marshall, *City of Gold and Mud. Painting Victorian London* (New Haven, CT: Yale University Press, 2012), Chapter 6.

children under 14 should only be emigrated if the receiving family were willing to pay for the passage and because demand for these children had declined, emigration to Canada almost ceased.[15] After this time, Australia became the biggest receiving country and the Middlemore Committee entered negotiation with the Child Emigration Society (more commonly known as the Fairbridge Society) in regard to children emigrating to Australia.[16] The Society had a farm school in Western Australia.

The CEH would take two or three parties consisting of 50–100 children to Canada either in early spring or in summer. The older boys would be settled to live with farmers and received around 30–60 dollars plus board and lodgings for their first year's service. The older girls were settled as domestic servants and received wages of about the same amount. The younger children were adopted and received board, lodgings and schooling. All employers and foster parents were, according to the annual reports, carefully selected.[17]

In 1873, on John Middlemore's first trip with the children, he accompanied 29 boys and girls to Canada. However, during this first journey, there was no receiving home until four weeks after arrival. Instead, the party of boys was housed in Newsboys Lodgings and the girls in a girls' home, and after an "advertising campaign" in the local newspapers, all children were settled.[18] In 1874, Guthrie Home was purchased and became the receiving home for the children. In 1898 Fairview Home was built in Nova Scotia, where the majority of children were received until the Canadian scheme ended in 1935. During those early trips to Canada, Middlemore would personally accompany the children and, with the help of the Hon. Mr Allan, Professor Wilson and Messrs Heath and Finnamore, settle the children.[19] Later, one or two members of the committee would accompany the children to Canada, where they would later be settled by the managers of the receiving homes. Unlike in Canada, where the children would be sent to work on farms or as domestic help, in Australia children were kept and trained in residential schools owned by the Fairbridge Society until they were of employment age.

The CEH estimated that it cost £16 to train a child in Birmingham and to find them a home in Canada. The Homes mainly relied upon the annual subscriptions of individuals, churches, Sunday schools and businesses in the Birmingham area, but also received financial support from America – where donations came in from Boston, Massachusetts, where John Middlemore had worked – and from Canada.[20]

---

[15] J. Eekelaar, "'The Chief Glory': The Export of Children from the United Kingdom"*Journal of Law and Society* 4, no. 21 (1994): 487–504.

[16] CEH, *Fifty Third Annual Report* (Birmingham, 1925). The Child Emigration Societywas established by Kingsley Fairbridge in Oxford in 1909. Fairbridge, influenced by Barnardo, wished to establish a farm school overseas. Unable to establish one on Canada, he looked to Western Australia. A small farm was purchased in Pinjarra to which children from England were taken. The aim was to train boys for farm work and girls to be domestic servants, but also to promote Commonwealth migration all over the British Empire. The scheme had very influential supporters in the Prime Minister, Stanley Baldwin; the Duke and Duchess of York (King George VI and Queen Elizabeth); and the Prince of Wales (Edward VIII). For further detail on Kingsley Fairbridge and the Farm Schools, see Roger Kershaw and Janet Sacks *New Lives for Old: The Story of Britain's Child Migrants* (London: National Archives 2008).

[17] CEH, *Nineteenth Annual Report* (Birmingham, 1891).

[18] P. Roberts-Pichette (n.d.), "John Throgmorton Middlemore and the Children's Emigration Homes," http://www.bifhsgo.ca/upload/files/Articles/JohnThrogmortonMiddlemoreAndThe ChildrensEmigrationHomes.pdf (accessed June 20, 2012).

[19] Ibid.

[20] CEH *Twenty-Sixth Annual Report* (Birmingham, 1898).

Donations also included bed sheets, shirts, socks, flannel vests, cake, Christmas cards, pinafores, stockings, skirts, sweets, toys, dripping, firewood, apples, jam, cuffs, marbles, caps, dolls and scripture texts.[21] As well as relying on subscriptions, donations and gifts in kind, the CEH distributed collecting cards and boxes, to give to anyone who asked for them.[22]

By 1892, 20 years after its founding, the CEH had received 2209 boys and girls, of whom 2049 had been taken to Canada.[23] From 1925 until the end of the Canadian scheme, the numbers of children sent to Canada began to dwindle. In 1926, for example, only eight were sent; instead, the CEH looked to Australia to receive their children. In the first year of the Australian scheme, four boys were sent to Fairbridge Farm School in Western Australia. By 1936, the CEH had sent 5550 boys and girls to Canada and Australia.[24]

Evidence

This case study is based on data extracted from 78 annual reports produced by Middlemore Emigration Homes between 1873 and 1950. The reports constitute part of the collection belonging to what was Birmingham Reference Library, which was opened in 1866 as a space "through which should flow, and in which should be shaped, all the highest, loftiest, and truest ends of man's [sic] intellectual and moral Nature".[25] The library was not a subscriber, but it was not uncommon practice for Birmingham societies to deposit a copy of their reports and proceedings in the Reference Library. The reports have at different times been bound into a series of volumes. In the library catalogue, the reports are grouped together with other Birmingham reports and journals relating to welfare issues. The structure of the reports changed over the years, from a basic one of approximately 20 pages long with scant details to a more detailed report of approximately 55 pages long, which from 1890 included photographs. These are photographs from Canada of children who had been sent there previously. Between 1873 and 1944, a core set of headings was used in the annual reports:

- Object and method;
- Statistics;
- Description of the voyage;
- Description of the journey to the home;
- Acknowledgement of Birmingham and Canadian/Australian friends;
- List of subscribers (with often a special plea to local churches and Sunday Schools);
- List of contributions and donations received.

---

[21] CEH, *Thirteenth Annual Report* (Birmingham, 1885).
[22] CEH, *Twenty Fifth Annual Report* (Birmingham, 1897).
[23] CEH, *Twentieth Annual Report* (Birmingham, 1892).
[24] CEH, *Sixty Fourth Annual Report* (Birmingham, 1936).
[25] George Dawson, MP for Birmingham, quoted in Capel Shaw, "The Birmingham Free Libraries," in *Birmingham Institutions*, ed. J.H. Muirhead (Birmingham: Cornish Brothers Ltd, 1911), 414. The reports are now housed in the Library of Birmingham, which opened in September 2013.

In 1895, the first "before" and "after" photographs started appearing – one photograph depicting the child on entering the CEH in "rags" and the second showing an improvement in the dress and demeanour of the child after several months' training in the home (see Figs. 1–6). This is some 25 years after Dr Barnardo had commissioned "before" and "after" photographs as a means to raise funds for Barnardo Homes, a practice which later led to a court case and accusations of dishonesty and "artistic fiction".[26] There is no information as to whether the CEH had a Photographic Department such as the one Barnardo had established in his Home for Destitute Lads in 1871 or if, again as with Barnardo's, the CEH systematically photographed, as part of a procedure, all of the children "to obtain and retain an exact likeness of each child and enable them, when it is attached to his [sic] history, to trace the child's career".[27]

There are also photographs of children settled in Canada after a number of years (see Figures 7–10). All of these photographs are accompanied by some biographical information relating to the individuals caught on camera. By 1921, these "before" and "after" photographs had disappeared to be replaced by photographs sent from Canada of children working on farms, marriages of past Middlemore children and the homesteads of past Middlemore children. Only a few photographs came from Australia; instead, the focus increasingly became the children at play or work in the homes in Birmingham. Furthermore, no photographs appeared at the height of the Second World War. Table 1 presents a typology of the photographs found in the reports between 1890 and the Second World War.

Texts

The reports describing the work of the CEH regularly established a dialogue with subscribers and supporters by directly addressing them as "our readers" and by presenting them with memorable anecdotes. For example, the following anecdote is from the 1876 annual report and involves John Middlemore:

> As to my *mulatto boy*, a gentleman who was once a Birmingham town missionary met us last May at Toronto, when on our way to London Ontario. "shall you settle your children easily" he enquired of me. I told him that I feared that my little mulatto boy must remain at our Canadian home for a year or two. "if that be the case", he said, "I am willing to adopt him if you consider my home as a suitable one." Thus these children, three of them physically deformed, and the fourth not of our race, have left Godless and depraved homes in England for bright and Christian ones in Canada.[28]

The reference to the redeeming power of good Christian homes, and particularly the love of a good Christian woman, abound in the texts. Such references were also commonplace in contemporary literature about the lives of urban waifs.[29]

The quality of all of the photographs as they are reproduced in the reports is generally poor (as can be seen below), a fact acknowledged in England by the CEH: "we rarely succeed in getting good reproductions from our photographs". Nevertheless, the CEH believed the photographs "explain and illustrate our work as words

---

[26]Tagg, *Burden of Representation*, 84–5.
[27]Ibid., 83.
[28]CEH, Fourth Annual Report Birmingham, 1876), 6–7.
[29]Davin, "Waif Stories," 67–70.

Table 1. Categories of photographs in the archives

Location UK	Where	Who/What	Year
Before and After	The Homes	Single child or siblings	1895–1914 1916–1921
The Homes	The grounds or indoors	Group picnics, bathing pool, girls in home, boys in home, the dining hall, bathroom, dormitory	First appearance 1925
At School	Usually of school plays	Group photograph of Christmas plays, the playground, football team	First appearance 1925
Out of the Homes	Picnic, stroll in the Park		First appearance 1932
En route	On board the ship/about to embark	Party of girls, party of boys, mixed party	First photograph of party of boys and party of girls 1906, duplicated several times
The Homes		The nursery, Babies' Home, Children's Emigration Home	First photograph 1898
Location Canada			
After several years in Canada	In home	Children, children with new family, as adults	First photographs appear 1891. Reappear 1904
At work	On the farms	Boys in field, boys with horses	First appearance 1916
Homestead	Picture of the house	Homestead with or without people	First photograph appears 1911
The Home		Guthrie House	First photograph 1898
Location	**Australia**		
The Farm School	In the grounds	Eight photographs	1933

cannot do" and "illustrate our work ... [for] our readers in a thoroughly comprehensible way".[30]

The "before" and "after" images are repetitive in form: a full-length portrait of the isolated individual child, staring direct to camera and identified only by their first name and the first initial of their surname. Both are studio photographs (see the paired Figures 1–2, 3–4 and 5–6). In the former the setting is very basic, but in the latter their material wellness is attested to by the use of studio props. The "before" photographs represent the children as objects of neglect which rendered them "victims" and hence fit objects of charity; also, unlike adults, it indicated they had the potential for transformation. The "after" images were carefully constructed to project a transformation of both body and state of mind. The dirt of poverty was removed to reveal the saved child. In these "before" photographs, the setting is such that there is a gloom and barrenness in the backdrop, which reinforces the sense of the child's isolation and poverty. The girl is wearing shoes; her brother has none. The contrast with the "after" photographs is significant as transformation has occurred; now there

---

[30] CEH *Twenty Fifth Annual Report* (Birmingham, 1897) 6.

are material objects around them and both boy and girl are wearing white smocks, reflecting light and symbolic of purity.

The two images of John H.P. are intriguing, as the setting for both pictures is the same. The contrast is interesting as his clothes are oversized in the "before" photograph and well-fitting in the "after", to give an indication that he has put on weight.

Such transformations were captured in words as well as in photographs (Figure 1) in order to ensure that the viewer correctly understood what was being represented:

> The little boy is only 5 years old, and is starved, squalid, barefooted, and ragged. His open mouth and inert stare betoken listlessness and numbness of mind. The corresponding portrait by it side was taken after he had been trained 4 months with us. Here his mouth is closed, and his expression is placid, happy, and intelligent. If left to the influence of his surroundings, nothing can be predicted of the poor child, as he appears in his first portrait, but wretchedness, gross stupidity, inertness and vice; while, as we see him in his second, all that is good may be hoped for in his future. How great is the change! And yet it has been wrought simply by the influence of a good and loving woman.

Transformation of the child was achieved not only through Christian love and charity, but also through

> ... [p]rompt obedience, a little drill, regular occupations, orderly games and happy evenings, causes the eyes to open and the mouth to close, changing the bearing of a child and add an inch or two to his stature, by completely changing his feelings and daily ideas.[31]

The biographical texts which accompanied the images employed a lexicon of descriptors. The "before" children were variously described with the terms "open mouthed", "vacant", "feeble", "neglected", "filthy", "verminous", "illegitimate", "filthy", "disgust", "abandoned", "wretched" and "deserted"; the "after" by their binary opposites: "self respecting", "intelligent", "happy", "loved", "strong", "able" and "fortunate". Image and words were intimately conjoined to signal future failures and successes.

The short biographies often included details of the child's family life before arriving at the CEH. As stated earlier, there was a level of anonymity; nevertheless, the image and the words together made public intimate details of tragic episodes of family life, a process that Ramey has rightly noted as an "act of exposure".[32]

The reports were a vehicle for display. The photographs enabled readers to see at first hand child poverty in the city, and in doing so they engaged in what Patrick Joyce referred to as "spectacular consumption".[33] The reader, through the agency of the reports, "consumed the experiences" of living as a vulnerable child in the industrial city and was in turn transformed into an urban spectator.[34] The photographs and their accompanying biographical information not only magnified the divide between the deserving and undeserving urban poor, but also made "real" or visible what was and what could be: the child of the undeserving poor could be not only saved, but "remade". Further, faced with reports and novels which drew attention to the grim realities of industrialisation and its impact on the poor, and in particular stories about

---

[31] CEH *Twenty Third Annual Report* (Birmingham, 1895), 7.
[32] Ramey, *Childcare in Black and White*, 5.
[33] Patrick Joyce, *The Rules of Freedom. Liberalism and the Modern City* (London: Verso, 2003), 195.
[34] Ibid., 189. See also Seth Koven, *Slumming. Sexual and Social Politics in Victorian London* (Princeton: Princeton University Press, 2004).

the underclass of children known as the "street Arabs", the reports reassured middle-class readers by presenting a rhetoric of proof. Koven (2004) has argued that such images, if circulated beyond the middle and professional classes, stimulated in the poor a "desire for moral and physical elevation".[35] The photographs from Canada speak to the viewer in terms of success, a new life made good – a success not only for the child but also for the colony, as the Thirty-Seventh (1909) report made clear: "Is it not as good for the Empire, for Canada to gain such a family, as for Birmingham to lose one little slum child".[36] It is only very occasionally that reader is presented with any facts which signal failure of the migration scheme, and these are usually embedded within the statistical returns – for example, the number of children who died or those who could not adjust to the rural environment of Canada, with their journey of child migration consequently ending in the insane asylum.

Travel and translation

Images travelled to England from Canada and, to a much lesser degree, from Australia. It is clear that some were produced by foster parents and others by CEH visitors, but their production generally remains unclear. While the images moved from the frontiers of empire to the metropolitan centre, it also remains unclear whether the photographers had any knowledge of the use that would be made of their images in the annual reports, or, indeed, if the reports themselves travelled from the centre to the periphery.

Green Lewis (1996) noted that the appetite for gathering, collecting, taking and reading cultural signs had "no purer expression in the nineteenth century than photography" and as technology it was "far more widely regarded as an instrument of revelation than of deceit".[37] Sontag (2003) also noted the photograph is a way "of making 'real' matters that the privileged … might prefer to ignore".[38] These real matters were carried by the power of photography to objectify the subject, individuate them and present them in the form of a document.[39] The CEH annual reports presented through word and image a factual record of the organisation's activities.

Finally, how did these "factual" annual reports travel? As Morgan notes, "facts travel well when they travel with integrity; and when they travel fruitfully".[40] Yet what if the facts lack integrity? While the Barnardo photographic doctoring has already been mentioned, there is also evidence that all was not as it appeared for some Middlemore emigrants.

As stated earlier, the annual report of 1891 noted that older boys would receive around 30–60 dollars plus board and lodgings for their first year's service, while the older girls were settled as domestic servants and received about the same wages. The report from the following year changed the starting salary 20 dollars.[41] Yet Bagnall, in *The Little Immigrants: The Orphans Who Came to Canada*, writes of

---

[35]Koven, *Slumming*, 114.
[36]CEH, *Thirty-Seventh Annual Report* (Birmingham, 1909).
[37]Jennifer Green Lewis, *Framing the Victorians: Photography and the Culture of Realism* (New York: Cornell University Press, 1996), 2–3.
[38]Susan Sontag, *Regarding the Pain of Others* (FSG Books: New York, 2002).
[39]Tagg, *Burden of Representation*, 83–5.
[40]Mary S. Morgan, "Travelling Facts," in *How Well do Facts Travel?*, ed. Howlett and Morgan, 10.
[41]CEH, *Twentieth Annual Report* (Birmingham, 1892).

MODES AND MEANING: DISPLAYS OF EVIDENCE IN EDUCATION

Figures 1–4 Before and after photographs of brother and sister Ellen and Johnny G. Source: CEH, Twenty-Fifth Annual Report (Birmingham, 1897).

Annie Smith, who was shipped out in 1928 by the CEH. It was agreed that she would be paid eight dollars, four of which would be put in the bank until she was old enough to claim it, with three dollars sent to the home as its share and one dollar as her spending money. When she left the farm and asked for the money, she was given nothing because the woman she worked for blamed her for breaking dishes, cracking lamp chimneys and wasting food. She heard references to herself described as "trash" and by the woman she worked for as "poor trash." She would often hear

Figure 5–6 Before and after photographs of John H.P. Source: CEH, Twenty-Third Annual Report (Birmingham, 1895).

MARY ANN J., AFTER FIVE YEARS IN CANADA (SEE PAGE 6).

Figure 7 Photograph of Mary Ann J. after five years of living in Canada. Source: CEH, Thirty-Second Annual Report (Birmingham, 1904).

assertions that British peopkle were dirty and lazy.[42] Horace Weir, who was shipped over to Canada in 1924, was paid 10 dollars a month in 1931 for farm work for nine months. When he went to collect his wages, in order to go in search of his brothers and sisters, he was refused his earnings. A member of staff from the CEH in Canada then went to try and get the money, and they were also refused. Horace was told he should forget about his wages. He did find his brother and sister, but discovered that

---

[42]K. Bagnall, *The Little Immigrants: The Orphans Who Came to Canada* (Oxford: Dundurn Group, 2001), x.

Figure 8–9 Sisters Rose Annie and Fanny Evelyn E. and William B. living in Canada. Source: CEH, Thirty-Seventh Annual Report (Birmingham, 1909).

too much had changed and he no longer had a family.[43] There are also well-documented stories of neglect and abuse which challenge the integrity of the facts presented in the reports. Bean and Melville (1989) document a number of accounts from adults who had been emigrated as children. One recalls coming home from school one day to see the furniture in the yard and the house locked up:

> They had not paid the rent. I ended up in Middlemore Homes. I never saw my mother and father again, though I wrote to my mother. I was not asked if I wanted to go to Canada. There was no choice: you went in [to Middlemore] and stayed there until they had a bunch ready to go over.[44]

---

[43] Ibid, x.
[44] P. Bean and J. Melville, *Lost Children of the Empire* (London: Unwin Hyman, 1989), 136–7.

Figure 10 Ex-CEH girl Mrs. S. in Canada with her family. Source: CEH, Forty-First Annual Report (Birmingham, 1913).

Accounts also highlight the withholding of children's files. One child who had been sent to Australia in 1939 through the Fairbridge Society told Bean and Melville (1989): "I was sent out here knowing absolutely nothing about my relations. I was determined to find out if I had a mother and father and perhaps sister. But Fairbridge told me nothing."[45]

Eventually, when he was 53, he was sent his birth certificate by the Society and, through a genealogical society, discovered his mother's death (see Figures 1–4, 5–6, 7, 8–9, 10).

---

[45] Ibid., 155.

Case 2: The Dragon's Teeth: recognition and respect in 1970s Liverpool
Context

As a maritime and trading city, Liverpool has a long history of migration and intimate connections with the history of migration and with the two historical episodes that were to become so important to modern migration memory in the United Kingdom: the Great Famine in Ireland and the development and eventual abolition of both plantation and domestic slavery.[46] The famine story has been remembered partly through the growth of Liverpool's nineteenth-century Irish community and its impressive array of religious, cultural and educational facilities, which left an important legacy, even as the scale and pace of migration from Ireland slowed during the first part of the twentieth century and slum clearances ended the residential segregation of the city's "green half". As John Belchem has shown, the emergence of the hyphenated Liverpool-Irish identity that was increasingly articulated and celebrated in local heritage made the Irish an integral part of the city's official history and its popular memory.[47]

The same was not true for Liverpool's black community. Unlike in both Birmingham and London, the majority of the city's black communities were long-time residents – especially in the Liverpool 8 area, where pockets of severe deprivation tended to be overlooked by official concentration on the problems allegedly posed by the psychology and behaviour of mixed-race Liverpudlians. Social scientist Patrick McNabb, for example, certainly regarded mixed-race heritage as a disability, and he argued, in heavily racialised terms, that they suffered from "a thorough-going ambiguity in their emotional life" that made them a "dangerous population".[48] This kind of judgement was typical in that it ignored Liverpool's involvement in the slave trade, denied a long history of black settlement in the city and framed discussion of contemporary social problems around an individualised psychology that ignored the actual events and the legacies of the past.[49]

Ignoring slavery was made easier by those academic texts published in the 1950s that continued to insist that Africa benefited from the "revolutionary stimulus of an advanced culture that she obtained from Europe" and that the contact established and developed through slavery and colonialism was, despite the suffering

---

[46] For comment and analysis on public memory see, respectively, Cormac Ó Gráda, "Making Irish Famine History in 1995," *History Workshop Journal* 42 (1996): 87–104; Catherine Hall, "Remembering 1807: Histories of the Slave Trade, Slavery and Abolition", *History Workshop Journal* 64 (2007): 1–5.

[47] John Belchem, Irish, *Catholic and Scouse: The History of the Liverpool-Irish, 1800–1939* (Liverpool: Liverpool University Press, 2007).

[48] Patrick McNabb, "Integration in Liverpool: A Definition of the Problem," *Select Committee on Race Relations and Immigration: The Problems of Coloured School-Leavers* (London: HMSO, 1969), 813–28. Space makes it necessary to leave to one side debates about the definition and status of race but our starting point, and our interest in race ideas and propositions, is informed by Bob Carter, *Realism and Race. Concepts of Race in Sociological Research* (London: Routledge, 2000).

[49] Kevin Myers, *Struggles for a Past: Migrants and their Histories in Postwar Britain* (Manchester: Manchester Univesity Press, forthcoming).

caused, beneficial.[50] Indeed, an official history of Liverpool published in 1957 spoke of the civilising benefits of slavery on those who were owned and disciplined by slave masters.[51] It was said over and over again that Liverpool had a proud history of welcoming strangers and that, even if there were sometimes problems, these were always temporary. Liverpool, it was repeatedly claimed, had a history of tolerating immigrants and there was no race problem in the city.[52]

Community Relations Councils (CRC), or Voluntary Liaison Committees as they were known between 1965 and 1968, like the one in Liverpool, were established in most of the large towns and cities in England in the period around 1965–1975. Political scientists and sociologists have tended to dismiss the emergence of CRCs as an attempt by dominant political parties to create a racial buffer designed to protect the political establishment from black people's demands for fundamental social and political change.[53] By co-opting local black leaders, by articulating a rhetorical commitment to racial integration and by supporting a social welfare approach to migrant and minority communities, the argument has been that CRCs prevented the development of black consciousness and depoliticised the explosive question of race. Applied to the structures of formal politics, to the continued existence of racism or to questions about the distribution of material resources, these arguments may be persuasive. However, they are less convincing when applied to issues around "recognition, respect and honour" which, argues sociologist Göran Therborn, "constitute a major existential dynamic of human relationships, from urban street encounters to large imaginary communities".[54] It is around these questions of recognition and respect that the CRCs, and their neglected educational functions, can be seen as significant. CRCs were, after all, established as public education and campaigning bodies and, championing the idea that racialism was a form of cultural intolerance, were committed to a course of educating away "prejudice". The record of the CRCs in fulfilling these commitments was certainly erratic because, as local bodies, they were sensitive to different levels of political will, to the variable composition of local committees and to different local histories of immigration. However, and even when these kind of conditions appeared to be unfavourable, CRCs could wield significant influence precisely because they were a site where critical voices could begin to move the frontiers of the national imagination. In supporting shared reading and discussion, publishing and displaying educational texts and arranging for the travel of these texts across national boundaries, CRCs helped to address some of the

---

[50]Eric. G. Harrot, "Africans and Europeans," *Times Literary Supplement*, April 29 1955, 192.
[51]The defence of slavery is in George Chandler, *Liverpool* (London: Batsford, 1957) and discussed by Roger Anstey in *The Atlantic Slave Trade and British Abolition* (Atlantic Highlands: Prometheus Books, 1975). The denial of discrimination is reported in various sections of John Belchem, ed., *Liverpool 8000: Culture, Character and History* (Liverpool: Liverpool University Press, 2006) 386, 442.
[52]For evidence of the claim and some comment on it see, for example, Edward H. Patey, *My Liverpool Life* (London: Mowbray, 1983), 124–33. For a stimulating discussion on national cultures of tolerance see D. Feldman, "Why the English Like Turbans: Multicultural Politics in British History," in *Structures and Transformations in Modern British History*, ed. D. Feldman and J. Lawrence (Cambridge: Cambridge University Press, 2011), 281–302.
[53]For a synoptic review based on empirical data see Anthony M. Messina, "Mediating Race Relations: British Community Relations Councils Revisited," *Ethnic and Racial Studies* 10, no. 2 (1987): 186–202.
[54]Göran Therborn, *The World. A Beginner's Guide* (Cambridge: Polity, 2011), 94.

silences of dominant national narratives.[55] In doing so CRCs, or at least some of the people who worked for them, helped to develop the political and educational discussions about the constitution of multicultural societies that became a characteristic of many late twentieth-century European societies.

Evidence

In seeking to "further good citizenship in a multiracial society" and "advance the education of the inhabitants of Merseyside", the CRC in Liverpool made some tentative interventions in public education. Some of these were outlined in the Annual General Meeting held in June 1972 in which projects indicative of the cautious and conservative approach to be taken were evident. In the discussion on youth and employment it was decided to develop classes for young people in the "History and culture of different national groups in Liverpool that could be taught in out-of-school classes for young people, run by different national associations".[56] These kinds of suggestions for integration workshops for different national groups were common in this period. Undoubtedly well-meaning and impeccably liberal, they were also entirely inappropriate in Merseyside, where inward migration had largely stopped in the post-war period. Of much more significance, but also much more unusual, were the recommendations made by educationalists.

At the Annual General Meeting of LCRC in 1972, the creation of a reading group was announced. The purpose of the group was to examine racial attitudes in books, and especially textbooks, in common use, and both the aims and the organisation of the group owed much to Dorothy Kuya. Kuya was a community relations officer born and raised in Liverpool with an African and communist father who had been influential in the trade union organisation of merchant seamen in Liverpool in the 1940s.[57] One part of Kuya's childhood milieu was a working-class communism inflected by the specifically transnational experiences of immigrant merchant seamen, in which there was a strong cultural and educational ethos.[58] Seaman communist activists not only read the party newspaper and discussed party tracts; they also brought with them the ideas, and sometimes the texts, circulating in other parts of the world.

Their long-term influence was probably more pedagogical than ideological. In Liverpool, and at least in the context of community relations, it was the shared reading groups and the ethos of collective learning as a form of consciousness-raising that a generation of activists – communist, trade union and pan-African – would

---

[55]Krijn Thijs, "The Metaphor of the Master: 'Narrative Hierarchy' in National Historical Cultures of Europe," in *The Contested Nation: Ethnicity, Class, Religion and Gender in National Histories*, ed. Stefan Berger and Chris Lorenz (Basingstoke: Palgrave Macmillan, 2008), 60–74.

[56]Liverpool Record Office [LRO], Liverpool Community Relations Council [LCRC], Minutes of the AGM 22 June 1972.

[57]Diane Frost, "Racism and Social Segregation: Settlement Patterns of West African Seamen in Liverpool since the Nineteenth Century," *Journal of Ethnic and Migration Studies* 22, no. 1 (1996): 85–95.

[58]Kevin Myers, Interview with Dorothy Kuya, July 23, 2008. From an extensive literature see the sometimes romantic but also evocative Raphael Samuel, *The Lost World of British Communism* (London: Verso, 2006).

apply to the political and social struggles of the 1960s and 1970s.[59] Their reading and their discussion exemplified an approach to the idea of "the present as history" of trying to understand contemporary conditions as the conjuncture of particular historical forces whose legacies continued in the present and which, more or less explicitly, challenged the chronologies and methodologies of conventional academic history.[60] It can also be argued that these reading practices were an important element in the construction of new kinds of historical distance in the post-war period.[61] Many radical reading groups sought a closer proximity with, and a new sensibility towards, events in the past. Against a powerful national master narrative, shared reading groups could explore, for example, a silent history of slavery, of rapacious British colonialism abroad, immigration to Britain and extensive domestic racism on local streets.[62] In doing so, reading groups could begin to challenge the legitimate forms of knowledge and identity that were embedded in school textbooks. History textbooks were particularly prominent in promoting dominant narratives and one reason for the success and significance of the LCRC reading group was that it was an early intervention in the history wars that were to become a feature of late twentieth-century public debate, particularly in countries with a history of imperialism.[63]

Technology played an important role in this process of education. The ability, still quite novel in the post-war period, to reproduce text quickly and cheaply through mimeograph technology enabled activists not only to find an authorial voice but also to begin to be published. As Steven Clay and Rodney Phillips have pointed out in their history of the "mimeo revolution", mimeo publishing was quick, could be undertaken without formal training and encouraged what they call "collaborative sociality"; small groups of likeminded people could join together to write, edit, publish, collate, staple and mail.[64] Bounded together in a joint enterprise, this was a relatively democratised means of technological reproduction. It encouraged the formation of social movements because it gave campaigning groups a concrete means of debating their objectives, developing their agendas and reaching their audiences. The fruits of this labour are now slowly becoming available in specialist archives.[65]

It is difficult, from the available fragmentary evidence, to estimate either the extent or the feel of these shared reading practices in Liverpool. What can be said

---

[59]C.J. Robinson, *Black Marxism: The Making of the Black Radical Tradition* (Chapel Hill: The University of North Carolina Press, 2000); Jessica Gerrard, "Self-Help and Protest: The Emergence Of Black Supplementary Schooling in England," *Race, Ethnicity and Education* 16, no. 1 (2013): 32–58.

[60]For an interesting comment on this moment see Richard Johnson, "Historical Returns: Transdisciplinarity, Cultural Studies and History," *Journal of Cultural Studies* 4, no. 3 (2001): 261–88.

[61]Mark Salber Phillips, "History, Memory and Historical Distance," in *Theorizing Historical Consciousness,* ed. Peter Seixas (Toronto: University of Toronto Press, 2004).

[62]Kevin Myers and Ian Grosvenor, "Birmingham Stories: Local Histories of Migration and Settlement and the Practice of History," *Midland History* 36, no. 2 (2011): 149–62.

[63]Stuart Macintyre and Anna Clark, *The History Wars* (Melbourne: Melbourne University Publishing, 2003). For specific textbook analysis see S.J. Foster and K.A. Crawford, *What Shall We Tell the Children? International Perspectives on School History Textbooks* (Greenwich, CT: Information Age Publishing, 2006).

[64]Steven Clay and Rodney Phillips, *A Secret Location on the Lower East Side: Adventures in Writing, 1960–1980* (New York: Granary, 1998).

[65]In London, for example, the George Padmore Institute, the Black Cultural Archives and the Archives of the Irish in Britain.

with some certainty is that by 1973 an independent survey had confirmed the importance of reading in the most deprived areas of Liverpool. University of Liverpool sociologist Ilene Mellish noted the local "overwhelming desire amidst the black community (but not limited to it and certainly not relevant only to it) to gain information about the history, literature, and culture of black people throughout the world. The quantity and sophistication of reading in this area and done by this community is great indeed".[66] Mellish proposed to further develop and formalise this reading activity by the establishment of a Liverpool 8 community college that would provide a

> full program of courses, seminars and events dealing with the history, literature, and culture of the African peoples and their descendents [sic] throughout the world, aimed at simply meeting the general interests of residents in the area, at exploring gaps in local history of significance and interest far beyond inner city Liverpool. (such as a history of African settlement in Liverpool ...)[67]

Kuya, who trained as both nurse and teacher before being appointed the first Community Relations Officer in Liverpool, was part of this environment.[68] Her instigation of a reading and study group in the pursuit of anti-racist education needs to be seen as part of this context. The core reading team of 12 people, described as "a multi-racial team of parents and teachers", looked at a selection of books from four local multi-racial schools and some of the "many hundreds" submitted on request by publishers. Texts could be read both individually and collectively, but the points raised from readings were then discussed at group meetings. The criticisms made of Derry and Jarman's *The Making of Modern Britain* (until recently widely available in public libraries) are instructive. The group criticised the sparse references to the slave trade, pointed to the omission of black immigrants in the sections dealing with migration, and recommended that the centuries-long growth of British communities of Chinese, African and West Indian origin be given much more prominence in accounts of the local and national past. Writing in the Merseyside Community Relations Council report for 1973, and providing an update on the progress of the reading group, Kuya argued that "Liverpool is a prime example of the 'sins of the fathers visiting the children'" and that:

> The neglect of the problems of the original Non-white immigrant has led to many difficulties of the present day English Born Black Community. Racial discrimination is not a new phenomenon which came to Liverpool with the wave of New Commonwealth Immigrants in the 60s. Racial Discrimination has operated throughout the long period of time that Black People have lived in the city and reflects ideas that have prevailed in our society for many hundreds of years. It has been so much of our life style that the white community has operated it without thought, and the Black Community on the whole have become complaisant about its own lack of opportunities.[69]

---

[66]LCRC, 60/2; I. Mellish, "Some Notes on Action Research in Liverpool," February 1973, p. 10.
[67]Ibid.
[68]Dorothy Kuya. Teacher, educationalist, community relations officer in Liverpool, 1970–1977.
[69]These quotations and information on Kuya's activities are in LRO, MCRC 75/2 Annual Report 1972–73.

Kuya's perspective clearly emphasised the importance of recognising and discussing Liverpool's particular history with regard to slavery and its legacies for both the black and white population in the city. She saw it as crucial to the development of the community that the CRC recognised young people as "self determining and self programming" and "provided a service to help in their search for identity". Kuya stressed that it was the role of the CRC to be involved in "all forms of community action in helping our youth to achieve equality in society and in meeting and coping with their social, economic and cultural needs".[70]

Travel and translation

Three things are significant here. The first is that the CRC reading group had effectively created a new reading space with new conventions.[71] Prior to the formation of the CRC reading group, anti-racist projects were largely confined to isolated school projects or radical political groups. Any attempt to discuss the omissions of national and local history was accused of being politically motivated, biased or, as Alderman Dawes of the Birmingham Education Committee bluntly put it, designed to teach the "supremacy of the black".[72] Whilst those accusations did not disappear, the CRC reading group created a space in which groups of activists and concerned citizens brought new kinds of empire stories to light. These stories were counterposed to, and read against the grain of, the official account of imperial domination. The silences of imperial texts began to be challenged and alternative causes of contemporary prejudice and racism were identified. This reading space helped make those causes more respectable and they opened up new learning opportunities.

The second point is that the analysis that emerged out of the reading group was significantly different, and more radical, than that often associated with community relations work. Implicitly, community relations work was organised around the idea that there was a problem of "adaptation" in British society which required adjustment on all sides of the community. So the purpose of historical research and historical narratives was to explain the arrival and identity of different ethnic groups. Such narratives usually identified a distinct and uniform culture that was alien to Britain, and which might require tolerance, understanding or, where it was deemed to be problematic, educational and social work intervention. But, as Kuya and the CRC report argued, there was relatively little post-war migration to Liverpool. What existed was a longstanding black community that was systematically exploited, as studies of housing provision, educational experience and employment had begun to show. Yet it took many years of long and often sharp struggles before official agencies were ready to acknowledge these structural issues. For many years the systematic racism facing Liverpool-born black people, and especially young black people, was either denied by common-sense racist ideologies or misinterpreted by (or transposed into) the emerging race relations paradigm in post-war Britain. The CRC report was highly significant precisely because it was able to translate the emerging

---

[76]Ibid.
[71]David N. Livingstone and Charles W.J. Whithers, "On Geography and Revolution," in *Geography and Revolution,* ed. D. Livingstone and C.W.J. Whithers (Chicago: University of Chicago Press, 2005): 1–23.
[72]Quoted in Ian Grosvenor, *Assimilating Identities. Racism and Educational Policy in Post 1945 Britain* (London: Lawrence & Wishart, 1997), 158.

language of multiculturalism into something meaningful and appropriate for the specific conditions of Liverpool.

Third, and perhaps most significantly, the Liverpool Community Relations Council had not just the respectability but the financial and cultural resources to begin to publicise and distribute their work. They published a pamphlet with the details of their analysis and distributed it widely. A much-praised exhibition highlighting the deficiencies of history and geography textbooks was mounted in the CRC offices in 1974. Originally planned to run for a week, the exhibition was reportedly overwhelmingly in demand and originally ran for three weeks in total. An explicit and early attempt to expand the traditional national master narrative with a more global

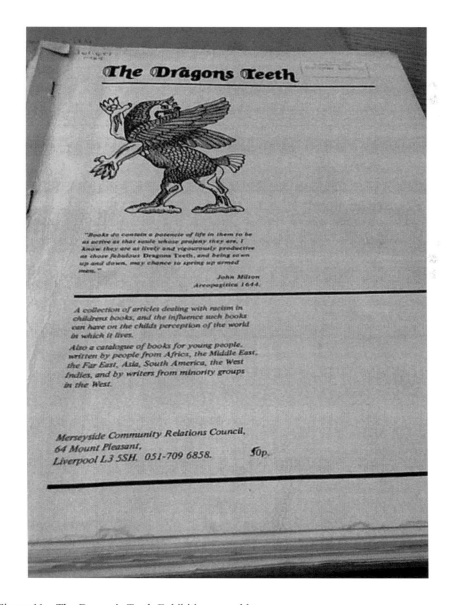

Figure 11   The Dragon's Teeth Exhibition pamphlet cover.

perspective, the exhibition attracted significant local attention, was reported in national and international news media and stimulated considerable comment and debate.[73] Judging from the admittedly limited evidence that attests to public responses to the exhibition, one of the most contested design features was a dustbin in which outdated and offensive texts were deposited, which generated discussion about censorship, unconscious attitudes and the legacies of British imperialism. The rejected books were "not very accessible or numerous", wrote one visitor, whilst another suggested that "the discard books which one finds unsuitable should be displayed also rather than put in bins, and show the reason".[74] In fact, the exhibition organisers and designers had faith in reason.

The accompanying booklet features a significant quotation from Milton's *Areopagitica* on the front cover. Writing in opposition to seventeenth-century press censorship and comparing the power of books to that of "Dragon's Teeth", Milton's text endorsed a renaissance humanism that was committed to dispelling myth and prejudice through a process of education that depended on the availability of relevant texts and the active interpretation of readers.[75] (See Figure 11[76]).

Reflections

In reflecting on our exploration in this paper of the CEH and CRC reports and the issues they raise for us as historians of education, we found Mary Morgan's recent essay "Travelling Facts" and Bill Schwarz's *White Man's World* particularly useful.[77] Morgan's essay is the product of a transnational research project that asked the question: "How well do facts travel?". Central to Morgan's answer, and to Schwarz's book, is a concern with exploring the dissemination of "reliable" and authoritative "knowledge". We have grouped our reflections under five headings – context of production; image and words; contexts of encounter; the historian's gaze; and technologies of production and display.

Context of production

Content is always produced within a specific context. This specificity is embedded in a particular historical conjuncture, a specific set of institutions and a specific discursive strategy. The content presented constitutes a form of shared knowledge for its community of readers, knowledge that the community will have "good reason to take ... as facts, and will be likely to have the confidence to act upon them as facts".[78] Content exists, in other words, within wider systems of representation and reform. The CEH and CRC reports both represent truths and both attest to a world

---

[73] LRO, LCRC, Minutes of the AGM 22 June 1972. For some indication of the controversies stimulated by the reading group analysis see the extended correspondence under the title "Little Black Sambo" in *The Times* newspaper, Monday 24 April 1972, 13; Wednesday 26 April 1972, 15; Thursday 27 April 1972, 17; Friday 28 April 1972, 15; Saturday 29 April 1972, 15; Monday 1 May 1972, 15; Tuesday 2 May 1972, 15 and Thursday 4 May 1972, 17.
[74] Liverpool Community Relations Council, *Sowing the Dragon's Teeth* (Liverpool: Liverpool Community Relations Council, 1974), n.p.
[75] Jonathan Rose, "The History of Education as the History of Reading," *History of Education* 36, 4–5 (2007): 595–605.
[76] Merseyside Community Relations Council, *The Dragon's Teeth Exhibition Pamphlet*, 1974.
[77] Morgan, "Travelling Facts," 3–39; Schwarz, *White Man's World*.
[78] Morgan, "Travelling Facts," 14.

of imperial authority. In the first case study, practical acts of charity (giving to the poor) were intimately connected to the imagined protection and extension of white civilisation. In the second section, the apparently reliable knowledge that underpinned imperial authority came under scrutiny and challenge. Though the case studies have different chronologies and time economies embedded in them, and different actors working on them, they are further evidence of the ways in which knowledge of empire conditioned educational practice and agency.

However, the procedures for establishing facts in the two different periods of our case studies were quite different. The CEH reports were produced in an era where production and publication were labour-intensive, required specialist knowledge and training, and so were relatively expensive. The CRC reports are themselves testimony to the increasing democratisation of facts and to a world in which a plurality of voices made claim to the facts of history. This has deeply affected historical practice because even if academic historians cling onto claims of objectivity and neutrality, and contrast their work with "political" or "emotional" claims, our case studies show that a different kind of register is needed to understand and explore historical evidence.[79] This is especially the case when historical claims function as an answer to the seemingly innocuous question "Where are you from?".[80] Indeed, the materials produced in both case studies are perhaps best understood not as "a monument to future memory" but as a "document for possible use".[81] In acting upon this knowledge, the community of readers/social actors can be understood to function as a "local disciplinary 'thought collective'".[82] Finally, this accepted knowledge has, through a mixture of agents and networks, the potential to connect with other clusters of knowledge and thereby reinforce its truth value.

Image and words

The two case studies both address the imagination and the very structures of feeling in metropolitan Britain. Peim has observed that looking (at visual and written texts) always has a subjective quality which shapes the ideas that are formed in dialogue with a text, and the meanings that are then constructed.[83] The first part of this paper focused on the ways in which meaning was extracted from images. However, the CEH reports consist of both images *and* words which, for the reader, are brought into dialogue with each other. Words, when used with images, can anchor meanings, as the photographer Dorothea Lange observed in the 1930s in her description of "pictures and words joined together in a kind of nurturing interdependence that illustrates the old aphorism that the whole is greater than the sum of its parts".[84] The difficulty for the historian, of course, is that of distance and the (im)possibility

---

[79]For analysis in terms of contemporary curriculum debates see Ian Grosvenor and Kevin Myers, "Engaging with History after Macpherson," *Curriculum Journal* 12, no. 3 (2001): 275–89.
[80]For the significance of the question, and the important insistence that identifications are always under review by thinking actors, see Schwarz, *White Man's World*, 15.
[81]Michel Foucault, *Discipline and Punish. The Birth of the Prison* (Aylesbury: Peregrine, 1977), 191–2.
[82]Morgan, "Travelling Facts," 14.
[83]N. Peim, "The History of the Present: Towards a Contemporary Phenomenology of the School," *History of Education* 30, no. 2 (2001): 177.
[84]Quoted in Ian Grosvenor and Ali Hall, "*Back to School from a Holiday in the Slums!*: Images, Words and Inequalities," *Critical Social Policy* 32, no. 1 (2012): 26.

of gauging the interrelationship between image and word in terms of how they structured the imagination and feelings of past readers. Acts of imagination and feelings, as well as emotions, images and symbols, are internal mental processes. As such, they pose difficulties for historians and their established evidential procedures even though they are frequently invoked by reference to attitudes, beliefs or intentions. So whilst recognising real difficulties with accessing internal mental processes, or what the sociologist Margaret Archer calls the "internal conversation", practices of self-talk or inner dialogue through which "agents reflexively deliberate upon the social circumstances they confront" are essential to the creation of meaning, and so too to the analysis of social change.[85] Symbols, images and emotions, as well as words on a page, all act as stimulants to internal conversations which are at once unique and context-dependent, and thus, crucially, open to investigation.

Where readers shared many of the same contextual references, as in the intended readership for the CEH reports, it is plausible to posit a shared mental landscape. The CEH presupposed and reflected a shared dominant narrative of imperial expansion, partly constituted by the biographies of settlers and by the geographies of an empire symbolised through a spread of philanthropic institutions. By way of contrast, the LCRC pamphlet and exhibition on *Sowing the Dragon's Teeth* are the outcome of experiences of contextual discontinuity brought about by migration, by the new international circulation of ideas and by racism. Many of the contributing members of the reading group were likely to have had similar feelings to Dorothy Kuya, who detested textbooks which "presented non-white people as living in primitive conditions and having no culture".[86] For much of the twentieth century this kind of realisation was a lonely experience, and one that was difficult to communicate. The LCRC reading group was significant precisely because it was a space in which elements of the internal conversation, the hurt and the shame induced by history textbooks, could be shared, and a language of criticism developed out of the individual responses to words, images, narratives and other kinds of organisational structures.

Contexts of encounter

David Livingstone has observed that knowledge begins at the point of encounter, and earlier in this essay we referred to the library as a site through which "flow" the "truest ends of man's intellectual and moral Nature".[87] It follows that making meaning of the "truest ends of man's intellectual and moral Nature" will be mediated through the spaces where that knowledge is encountered. It also follows that if we agree that the meaning[s] we take from the knowledge we encounter are always framed by the context in which we come upon them, then there is also need to examine and detail how that knowledge, for example in the form of photographs, reports, exhibitions and so on, travelled/entered into the space of encounter, and to consider its *circulation* and its *currency* as it moves through time and space from context to context.[88] Morgan refers to this as the "life histories" of "facts", which

---

[85]Margaret S. Archer, *Structure, Agency and the Internal Conversation* (Cambridge: Cambridge University Press, 2003), 130.
[86]Dorothy Kuya, "Little Black Sambo," *The Times*, May 1, 1972, 15.
[87]Livingstone, "Text, Talk and Testimony," 93–100.
[88]Ian Grosvenor, "L'álbum de l'escola: imatges, introspeccio i designualtats," *Educació i Història. Revista d' Història de l'Educació*, 15 (2010): 149–64.

need to be "traced and documented, examined, explained and understood".[89] This is particularly interesting in the case of the CEH reports as there is a second set of reports housed in the Central Library, but these arrived at a later date to the first set as part of the Middlemore Archive, a collection which also includes admission registers and individual child case files. This archive contains additional data related to the stories and images presented in the reports, data which would only have been seen by a select number of individuals involved in the organisation of the CEH. This data has the potential to challenge the integrity of the reports, especially through the content to be found in individual child case files. For example, in a letter book dated 24 September 1909, the Canadian manager refers to a letter from Victor J. Parr's mother, who was "spreading a report that her boy is being badly treated. [I] do not believe there is a word of truth in her statement".[90] This letter book was separate from the CEH annual reports and, more than likely, something only a select few would have witness of. Further, encountering the report in the archive as opposed to the library would be an encounter of a very different order. First, a researcher would be faced with an additional wealth of detail relating to the processes and procedures, the practicalities and personal experiences of the individual child's journey from home to Empire. Second, there is also the issue that the archiving archivist operates within a very different community of practice to the librarian. Finally, to further complicate the process of engagement with the past, there is in addition a further archive relating to the CEH which is held in Canada.[91]

The historian's gaze

Morgan (2011) usefully reminds us that "the facts that historians use have been addressed at some time past to other people in other places".[92] Making meaning, drawing historical insights, is contingent on acknowledging and understanding if possible the intention of the evidence creator at the moment of production, but also being willing and able to look for other possible disruptions, to elicit meanings which may be grounded in the document. Foucault advised: "Never consent to being completely comfortable with your own certainties."[93] The danger here is of being a too-"knowing" viewer, who looks but does not see. Knowing can be a barrier to seeing, a limitation on what otherwise are the fluid economies of meaning. Further, "knowing" is always accompanied by a particular form of understanding; as "human subjects" we "cannot be written out of the identity of the things that we see" – there is a subjective quality to our looking.[94] In the case of the migrant children we approached the reports (and the archive) with the full knowledge of the contested

---

[89]Morgan, "Travelling Facts," 12.
[90]Canadian Manager's Letter Book, September 24, 1909, Archived – Forging Our Legacy: Canadian Citizenship and Immigration, 1900–1977, www.collectionscanada.gc.ca
[91]http://www.cic.gc.ca/english/resources/publications/legacy/chap-2b.asp
[92]Morgan, "Travelling Facts," 32.
[93]Michel Foucault, "For an Ethics of Discomfort," in *The Politics of Truth: Michel Foucault*, ed. S. Lotringer and L. Hochroth (New York: Semiotexte, 1997), 144. See also Valerie Harwood and Mary Louise Rasmussen, "Studying Schools with an Ethics of Discomfort," in *Dangerous Coagulations, The Uses of Foucault in the Study of Education*, ed. Bernadette M. Baker and Katharina E. Heyning (New York: Peter Lang, 2004): 305–21.
[94]Peim, "The History of the Present," 177. Subjective here does not equate with a subjective individualism for reasons outlined by Archer in *Structure, Agency and the Internal Conversation*, especially chapters 3 and 4.

histories surrounding child migration to Canada and Australia and the public apologies made by the political leaders of Australia and the UK in 2009. This observation about "knowing" connects back to our first point about the context of production and how knowledge is a product of a specific moment and its meaning is linked to that moment, but it comes to us in the present divorced from that context of understanding. Indeed, it could be argued that the "after" images and those produced in Canada returned to the individuals concerned an element of dignity, to counter the "act of exposure". Similarly, the account of the CRC and the Liverpool exhibition, and the interpretation offered here, is reflective of the theoretical discussions over the past few decades which have moved historical scholarship away from a Eurocentric perspective and raised questions about subjectivities in history.[95]

Technologies of production and display

The changing technologies of production and display are an important theme of our paper, but still a neglected topic in the history of education.[96] Mimeo technology certainly helped to create a more democratic public space in Britain and elsewhere after 1945. It also very probably stimulated new forms of display in which authoritative knowledge was subject to reordering, challenge and contestation precisely because it was amenable to reproduction in new forms and contexts.

Finally, there is the issue of how the images we selected for this paper have travelled both from the repository into our academic paper and accompanying PowerPoint presentation, and finally into print. The vehicle in all cases has been digital technology. The images now exist on our computers and can be electronically circulated and/or placed on the web to be explored remotely online, where they can become free-floating signifiers, losing their identity as they are submerged in the single archive which is the internet.[97] The shift to digital accumulation and distribution systems has important consequences for the permanence and accessibility of the historic record. Items in this ever-expanding virtual archive of historical knowledge have no rarity value since they can be replicated "instantly, inexpensively and indefinitely" because of their digital format.[98] Further, new imaging technologies have also shifted the relationship between the real and the artificial, which will further complicate the issue of believability[99] and our search as historians for reliable knowledge.

---

[95]See the essays in Emily S. Rosenberg, ed., *A World Connecting 1870–1945* (Cambridge, MA: The Belknap Press, 2012).
[96]See Martin Lawn and Ian Grosvenor, eds. *Materialities of Schooling: Design, Technology, Object Routines* (Oxford: Symposium, 2005).
[97]Eric Margolis, "Class Pictures: Representations of Race, Gender and History in a Century of School Photographs," *Visual Sociology*, 14 (1999): 8–9.
[98]William. J. Mitchell, "*Wunderkammer* to World Wide Web: Picturing Place in the Post-Phtographic Era," in *Picturing Place. Photography and the Geographical Imagination*, ed. Joan M. Schwartz and James R. Ryan (London: I. B. Tauris, 2003), 302.
[99]See Fred Ritchin, *In Our Own Image: The Coming Revolution in Photography/How Computer Technology is Changing Our View of the World* (New York: Aperture, 1990).

Activism, agency and archive: British activists and the representation of educational colonies in Spain during and after the Spanish Civil War

Siân Roberts

School of Education, University of Birmingham, Birmingham, UK

> In the late 1930s the Spanish Civil War captured the international imagination to an extraordinary degree. As in other countries British men and women were moved to intervene directly and the memory of the war, and of British participation in it, has held an enduring appeal in the UK. The Civil War was also notable for its use of the visual as a weapon of propaganda, and the Spanish Republican Government deployed visual imagery to great effect as an instrument through which it exhibited its progressive educational and welfare reforms to an international audience. This article focuses on the visual and textual representations of displaced children in Republican educational colonies in Spain that are preserved in British archive collections. Taking as its starting point a series of photographs of children in colonies gathered together as part of the International Brigade Memorial Archive in London, the paper will consider the construction, use, and circulation of these images and associated texts by British and American political and humanitarian networks and their subsequent collection and preservation in British archival institutions. The paper will assess the effectiveness of the images and texts as pedagogical and political agents and explore how their meaning shifted as they travelled through a range of performative spaces on a journey from their construction as artefacts designed initially to record and communicate the Spanish Republic's progressive educational project, to commemorative objects in the archive.

Introduction

> Miss Lloyd Williams, who recently returned from a three weeks' visit to Spain, testified to the pitiable plight of refugee children deprived in many cases of both parents... Mr. Horace G. Alexander, local chairman of the Friends' Committee, also emphasised from his experience in Spain the needs of the children, and showed a number of lantern slides to illustrate the way in which problems of feeding and lodging were tackled.[1]

This quotation derives from a report in the local press in Birmingham, UK. It describes a gathering at the local Meeting House of the Religious Society of Friends (also known as Quakers) in Bull Street on the evening of 21 January 1937, one of many such gatherings that had been held in Birmingham and elsewhere since the

---

[1] *Birmingham Post*, January 21 1937, p. 6.

outbreak of the Spanish Civil War some six months earlier. The meeting's purpose was both to raise awareness of the conditions in Spain, particularly as they affected children, and to raise money for the relief effort.[2] As a description it captures two elements that are central to the focus of the article that follows – first the speakers' use of personal, eye-witness testimony intended to mobilise support for the relief effort, and second the use of the visual, in this case lantern slides, to "prove" the truthfulness of their accounts and to illustrate the transformative power of the relief effort.

It is this visual and textual representation of displaced children in Republican Spain by British humanitarian and political activists which is at the core of this study. It takes as its starting point a series of photographs purporting to depict the lives of children in a specific educational space – Republican educational colonies in Spain – which are gathered together as part of the International Brigade Memorial Archive in London (hereafter IBMA).[3] I will begin by exploring what is known of the construction of the images by the Spanish Republican authorities before going on to consider their circulation and use by British political and humanitarian networks. The images will then be considered alongside textual representations of the same educational spaces, in an attempt to situate the photographs within a broader discourse of humanitarian aid and political activism. In so doing I will draw on the model of social biography, agency and performativity of photographic images developed by Elizabeth Edwards to raise questions about their effectiveness as pedagogical and political agents, and consider their journey through a range of performative spaces across international boundaries.[4] The article will conclude with a consideration of the motivations behind their subsequent collection and preservation in a British archival institution before going on to explore how this latter stage in their biography influenced their meaning.[5]

Critical engagement with the visual is now an accepted discourse within both the history of education and the broader field of historical studies.[6] As a detailed

---

[2]On the British "Aid Spain" movement see Jim Fyrth, *The Signal was Spain: The Aid Spain Movement in Britain 1936–3* (London: Lawrence and Wishart, 1986); on British and American Quaker relief during the Civil War see Farah Mendlesohn, *Quaker Relief Work in the Spanish Civil War* (New York: The Edwin Mellen Press, 2002).
[3]For information on the archive and its contents see *International Brigade Memorial Archive: Catalogue,* Vols. 1–3 (London: Marx Memorial Library, 1986, 1990 and 1994).
[4]Elizabeth Edwards, *Raw Histories: Photographs, Anthropology and Museums* (Oxford: Berg, 2001).
[5]This paper is limited to sources for Spanish children's colonies in British archival institutions. Further exploration in Spanish archives would constitute a further stage of the research and would undoubtedly add considerably to our understanding of the issues.
[6]See for example Ian Grosvenor, Martin Lawn, and Kate Rousmaniere, eds., *Silences and Images: The Social History of the Classroom* (New York: Peter Lang Inc., 1999); *Paedagogica Historica* special issue 36, no. 1 (2000); *History of Education* special issue "Ways of seeing Education and Schooling: Emerging Historiographies," 30, no. 2 (2001); Nick Peim, "Spectral Bodies: Derrida and the Philosophy of the Photograph as Historical Document," *Journal of Philosophy of Education*, 39, no. 1 (2005): 67–84; U. Mietzner, K. Myers, and N. Peim, eds., *Visual History: Images of Education* (Bern: Peter Lang, 2005); *History of Education* special issue 36, no. 2 (2007); Ian Grosvenor, "From the 'Eye of History' to 'a Second Gaze': The Visual Archive and the Marginalized in the History of Education," *History of Education* 36, nos. 4–5 (2007): 607–22. Beyond the history of education see for example Peter Burke, *Eyewitnessing: The Uses of Images as Historical Evidence* (London: Reaktion Books, 2001); Peter Burke, "Interrogating the Eyewitness," *Cultural and Social History* 7, no. 4 (2010): 435–44.

discussion of this growing literature is beyond the scope of this article and has been comprehensively rehearsed elsewhere, it is sufficient for my purposes here to draw attention briefly to one or two of the main arguments that inform this study, in particular those relating to photography and the rhetoric of truth, and photography and the representation of war and conflict. A number of commentators across a range of historical disciplines have drawn attention to the immediacy and intimacy of photography and the resulting "expectancy of the real, the truthful".[7] John Tagg in particular problematised the "documentary" tradition, a discourse which was formed in the 1920s and came into its own in the 1930s, the period under study here. Tagg argued that the documentary "appropriated photographic technology to a central and privileged place within its rhetoric of immediacy and truth".[8] In his analysis of the growth and use of photography as a technology of knowledge, surveillance and power, he emphasised the context of production and deployment when analysing the visual. Building on Tagg's work, Caroline Brothers analysed the relationship between issues of truth and the photography of war, and of the Spanish Civil War in particular.[9] Brothers scrutinised the photographic representations of the war in the British and French press "not for what they literally depict so much as for how they were used, how their meanings were structured so they became elements of and stakes in the struggle instead of just witnesses to it".[10] She concluded that in the Spanish Civil War, photographs "became images not just *of* but *in* conflict".[11]

The images which form the starting point for this article are part of a group of 128 photographs gathered together as file D in box A2 of the IBMA, housed at the Marx Memorial Library in London. In addition to the specific photographs under discussion here, the file includes other images of Spanish children which will not be discussed in any detail, including photographs of model schools in Spain and a series of atrocity photographs of children killed and maimed in the conflict. The specific images upon which I intend to focus purport to depict the lives of displaced children living in Republican educational colonies. Colonies were developed by the Republican Government to provide for the care and education of large numbers of children displaced or evacuated from their homes during the Civil War. As with all movements of displaced people, it is difficult to accurately estimate the exact numbers involved, although one study estimates that by September 1937 over 45,000 children were being cared for in 564 colonies.[12] Contemporary accounts by relief workers at the time appear to confirm the scale of these numbers; an account written by five American social workers published in winter 1937, for example, estimated

---

[7] Edwards, *Raw Histories*, 9.
[8] John Tagg, *The Burden of Representation: Essays on Photographies and Histories* (Basingstoke: Palgrave Macmillan, 1988), 8.
[9] Caroline Brothers, *War and Photography: A Cultural History* (London and New York: Routledge, 1997). On photographic representation and war see also Janina Struk, *Photographing the Holocaust: Interpretations of the Evidence* (London and New York: I.B. Tauris and Co. Ltd, 2004).
[10] Brothers, *War and Photography*, 3.
[11] Brothers, *War and Photography*, 2, emphasis in the original.
[12] Michael R. Marrus, *The Unwanted: European Refugees in the Twentieth Century* (New York: Oxford University Press, 1985); "El Exilio Español de la Guerra Civil: Los Niños de la Guerra," www.ugt.es/fflc/ninos00 (accessed April 3, 2005); A.L. Geist, and P.N. Carroll, *They Still Draw Pictures: Children's Art in Wartime from the Spanish Civil War to Kosovo* (Urbana: University of Illinois Press, 2002), 17.

that 60,000 children were living "in colonies or semi-colonial groups" at that point in time.[13]

The colonies were established and administered under the direction of the Republican Ministry of Education by a number of Spanish relief and voluntary organisations, often supported by international activists and relief agencies such as the Society of Friends and Save the Children.[14] They were organised in requisitioned houses, or groups of houses, where between 25 and 100 boys and girls up to 15 years old were to be cared for, educated and given medical attention as required. The intention was to replicate as closely as possible "a homelike atmosphere; [and] to treat each child with the same care and the same affection as would be given him [sic] by his own parents".[15] The colonies were popular destinations for visits by foreign activists and relief workers whose accounts suggest that on the whole they were of a high standard, although as the war progressed and supplies became increasingly difficult to obtain, conditions inevitably worsened.[16] The quality of the images in the IBMA file varies considerably: some appear to be snapshots taken by foreign visitors, whilst others have been professionally produced using good-quality equipment. Contextual information is scarce; the name of the colony is known, or guessed, in only a few instances and individual children are not named. Furthermore, many of the photographs are stuck firmly to loose-leaf pages in a binder, thereby obscuring any original captions or information on the reverse.

In contrast to the atrocity photographs also found in the file, the beauty and intimacy of some of the photographs of schools and colonies is striking, and it is not hard to appreciate their power as fundraising and publicity images. Indeed, when I first looked at the two photographs reproduced here as Figures 1 and 2 I was profoundly conscious of being manipulated both by their beauty and by their sense of intimacy, as well as by the clever use of recognisable documentary photographic techniques from the period. Scanning quickly through the images I was drawn by the gaze of the pretty little girl who is the central focus of the photograph reproduced here as Figure 1.[17] Closely watched by two other little girls, she is the only one of the children who returns the photographer's gaze, with a look that is both

---

[13] Child Care Commission of the Social Workers Committee to Aid Spanish Democracy, "Case Record of New Spain," *Social Work Today*, November 1937, 9–11 and December 1937, 21–22.

[14] The Spain files of the Friends Service Council at the Friends Library, London, document a number of colonies and their administering organisations, including Asistencia Infantil, Pro Infancia Obrera, and Ayuda Infantil de Retaguardia. File FSC/R/SP/1/3, for example, includes a report by Rica Jones on children's colonies in the province of Gerona [April] 1937.

[15] National Council for Evacuated Children, Ministry of Public Education, Spanish Republic, *Children's Colonies* (Valencia, November 1937), IBMA Box A/5, File A/8, p. 7.

[16] For information on the British activist Francesca Wilson and her visits to children's colonies in Spain see Siân Roberts, *Place, Life Histories and the Politics of Relief: Episodes on the Life of Francesca Wilson, Humanitarian Educator Activist*, PhD diss., University of Birmingham, 2010, chapter 4; Francesca M. Wilson, *In the Margins of Chaos: Recollections of Relief Work in and between Three Wars* (London: John Murray, 1944). For other accounts see also Jim Fyrth and Sally Alexander, *Women's Voices from the Spanish Civil War* (London: Lawrence and Wishart, 1991); Cambridge University Library, Helen Grant Papers, MS ADD 8251/II, typescript report on Spain.

[17] IBMA Box A/2, File D/17.

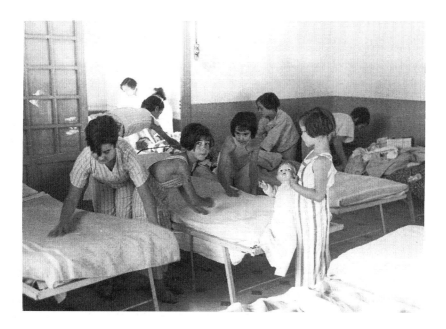

Figure 1. Girls at an unidentified colony (courtesy of the International Brigade Memorial Archive, Marx Memorial Library).

curious and knowing, displaying an acute awareness "of being looked at".[18] I turned the page and was entranced by the sunlight falling on the faces of the three boys in Figure 2.[19] All three are laughing at something, or someone, beyond the frame of the image; their clothing, facial expressions, comradely body language and the rural background all suggest a healthy, hardworking and happy life. Both photographs appear to be part of a series taken at an unidentified colony and stylistically have a very different feel to many of the others in the file, which are more akin to snapshots taken by activists. If removed from the archival frame of the IBMA file, nothing in their internal composition would indicate that they are photographs of children displaced from home and family by a brutal civil war. The overwhelming impression given is of a succession of happy and healthy children living in beautiful surroundings and engaging in a daily round of lessons, meal-times, communal chores, cultural activities and play, albeit in an institutional setting.

On one level, therefore, these photographs can be read as a representational portrait of daily life and activities in the colonies. However, they have a sense of agency and performative intent that goes far beyond a factual representation of the day-to-day. Several commentators have emphasised the multi-vocal nature of images and the need to look to the context of their construction when exploring their multiple and often conflicting interpretations.[20] As stated earlier, what lay beyond the

---

[18]Diane Waggoner, "Photographing Childhood: Lewis Carroll and Alice," in Marilyn R. Brown, ed., *Picturing Children: Constructions of Childhood between Rousseau and Freud* (Aldershot: Ashgate, 2002), 149.
[19]IBMA Box A/2, File D/18.
[20]J. Evans and S. Hall, eds., *Visual Culture: The Reader* (London: Sage, 1999), 309; Ian Grosvenor, "On Visualising Past Classrooms," in Grosvenor, Lawn, and Rousmaniere, *Silences and Images,* 91.

Figure 2. Boys at an unidentified colony (courtesy of the International Brigade Memorial Archive, Marx Memorial Library).

frame of these images was a war in which visual imagery was deployed as a weapon of propaganda by both sides to great effect, and this provides part of the context within which they should be read. As Brothers and others have argued, the Spanish conflict was the first war to be photographed for a mass audience and coincided with the growth of documentary photojournalism in the 1930s and its deployment by newly founded magazines such as *Life* (1936) and *Picture Post* (1938).[21] The Spanish Republic was very keen to promote its reputation for progressive educational and welfare reforms and the visual, including documentary photography and film, provided a key tool for communicating this message to an international audience; the Spanish Pavilion in the 1937 International Exposition in Paris, for example – popularly remembered for its inclusion of Picasso's *Guernica* – also deployed film and photography to strike a precarious balance between the conflicting objectives of enlisting sympathy for an embattled government and people on the one hand, and representing stability and modernity on the other. Images of educational and welfare activities were given pride of place, with images of children reading and scenes from the Pedagogic Missions of the early 1930s included in the external and internal displays as a means of "proving" the reality of Republican reforms.[22]

Reading the IBMA photographs against other archival sources illuminates their performative intent, and contributes to our understanding of their biography. In the same archive as the photographs is a pamphlet entitled *Children's Colonies* which consists of

---

[21] Brothers, *War and Photography*; B. Epps, "Seeing the Dead: Manual and Mechanical Spectres in Modern Spain (1893–1939)," in S. Larson and E. Woods, eds., *Visualizing Spanish Modernity* (Oxford and New York: Berg, 2005), 134; see for example the photo essay of images from the Spanish conflict by Capa in *Picture Post,* December 3, 1938.

[22] Jordana Mendelson, *Documenting Spain: Artists, Exhibition Culture, and the Modern Nation, 1929–1939* (University Park: Pennsylvania State University Press, 2005), 125–82.

recommendations for the establishment and administration of colonies, originally drawn up by the National Council for Evacuated Children, and published in French and English by the Spanish Delegation for Evacuated Children in Paris in November 1937.[23] The multilingual nature of the publication is in itself interesting and reflects not only the presence of numerous foreign relief workers in Spain, but again the Republic's desire to disseminate a progressive image to an international audience. A similar motive can be discerned in other sources for the period: Luis Buñuel's documentary film *Las Hurdes: Land Without Bread*, which depicted life in the Extremadura region and was originally made in 1933, for example, was edited with sound in French and English in December 1936 with funding from the Spanish Embassy.[24]

Children's Colonies makes very explicit the colony's role in inculcating specific patterns of normative behaviour in the children to produce a new type of citizen for the future. These behavioural patterns touched almost all aspects of the child's life, including health and hygiene, active citizenship, social interaction and cultural expectation. The document alludes to the importance of the visual as a means of communication, stating that the "publications, photographs and postal cards... bring out the constructive work realized in this realm by the Ministry of Education".[25] The patterns of behaviour it describes are reflected so closely in the IBMA photographs that they could almost have been produced specifically to illustrate the text. As space is limited here, I will touch on two key themes which underlie the whole educative process: the development of active citizenship within a collective, and the "civilising" benefits of training in aesthetic appreciation and personal hygiene.

The colony was to foster in the children an ethos of co-operative participation and personal responsibility within a collective framework:

> Care should be taken to organize the work of all the Colonies along cooperative lines, founded on the work which directly affects the collective. For example, with the girls, the bigger ones will help the smaller ones with their sewing, each taking over direction of one of them in making table linen, handkerchiefs, etc. All the children who are old enough will make their beds and clean their rooms and will do what has been assigned to them in the way of helping with the cleaning of the rest of the house. A weekly rotating schedule for waiting on tables should be drawn up. Whenever possible, work-teams should be formed to carry on the necessary work of the Colony – raising useful animals, agricultural work on the collective lands, construction or setting in order of necessary tools and furniture, laying in supplies, etc.
>
> In short, the whole life of the colony should be given a deep sense of cooperation, which will bring out the constructive and creative aspect of working in a group.
>
> In this way will be developed in the children the feeling for solidarity and mutual combining individual efforts to form a real working Community.[26]

This theme is consistently reflected in the images, which show groups of children working, learning and playing together. Although the colonies were co-educational,

---

[23] National Council for Evacuated Children, Ministry of Public Education, Spanish Republic, *Children's Colonies*, Valencia, November 1937, IBMA Box A/5, File A/8, p. 5. Another copy of this document can be found in the London School of Economics Archives (LSE), Spanish Civil War Collection, Misc. 91, volume 18/5, microfilm 513.
[24] Mendelson, *Documenting Spain*, 67.
[25] *Children's Colonies*, 3.
[26] *Children's Colonies*, 13–14.

as the above quotation and the anecdotal evidence of visitors suggests, on the whole the work was still arranged along a traditionally gendered pattern and this is also reflected in the images, with the girls undertaking housework, washing clothes and sewing and the boys engaging in agriculture, caring for animals and gardening. Occasionally there appears to be a conscious effort to present a different picture, with photographs of boys using sewing machines, for example.[27] Another way in which individual responsibility in a collective context was encouraged was through self-government by the children. This again is represented in the IBMA archive, which includes photographs of children participating in committees which played an active role in the running of the colony whilst at the same time providing an opportunity for political and citizenship education.[28] British activists visiting the colonies were very struck by this element of self-government, and remarked upon it; the Birmingham-based teacher and activist Francesca Wilson, for example, described "parliaments" where children as young as five gathered together to discuss and decide upon issues such as "a rearrangement of their lessons, the feeding of the chickens and rabbits, the assignment of domestic duties, the water supply".[29]

The second theme which emerges from *Children's Colonies* and which is again reflected in the images is that of training the children in the basic principles of personal hygiene and health, and the behavioural norms of a cultured and civilised life. The children, many of whom were reported as coming from very poor areas of cities such as Madrid and Malaga, were to learn that attention to cleanliness and aesthetic considerations were both an essential part of the human condition, even in the most difficult of circumstances:

> Whether the accommodations are luxurious or modest, the house should always have two characteristics: *cleanliness and good taste*. Arrange things so that even in the most rudimentary accommodations there will be some pleasing and attractive note such as a few simple pieces of pottery work or china produced in the vicinity, flowers, plants, a bookcase with books, etc. If the desire is there, means can be found to do this.[30]

Every care was to be taken to ensure that this lesson was reinforced through the design and furnishing of the colonies. The children's communal dormitories had to be attractive and comfortable, with bedspreads in "harmonious colours". This again is borne out by British visitors to colonies, who describe houses with light and airy rooms situated in beautiful gardens and repeatedly stress the cleanliness and attention to design. The British activist Helen Grant, for example, describes a colony where beds were "painted pale blue with designs of ducks or boats on them" and a dining room that was particularly attractive, "with yellow chairs and flowers everywhere".[31]

The organisation of the dining room was to reflect both the collective ethos and aesthetic and behavioural considerations; the children were to learn that tables were routinely adorned with attractive tablecloths and napkins (which the girls were

---

[27] See photograph D/40 in the IBMA, Box A/2. The Imperial War Museum (IWM) in London also holds a photograph of washing clothes at the Furnes "Republic of Free Refugee Children" in 1938, which in the original album is captioned "boys were made to share this work, which was regarded as most unusual" (Photographic Archive HU33143).
[28] For example photographs D/106 and D/107 in the IBMA, Box A/2.
[29] Wilson, *In the Margins of Chaos*, 198. See also Helen Grant Papers, Cambridge University Library MS ADD 8251/II, 36–37.
[30] *Children's Colonies*, 7–8 (emphasis in the original).
[31] Helen Grant Papers MS ADD 8251/II, 21–22.

encouraged to make) and that glasses were to be used for drinking. It was "necessary to accustom the children to using these things, and keeping them in good condition", and mealtimes were singled out as one of the most important opportunities for informal instruction so that "the good sanitary habits and the social training which grow out of these everyday tasks will be established".[32] Again the IBMA photographs illustrate these issues, with images of clean and well-dressed children sitting at their meals around beautifully arranged tables in cheerful, bright dining rooms.[33]

Children's Colonies places great emphasis on personal cleanliness and training in personal hygiene, stipulating, for example, how often the towels and bed linen should be washed:

> Particular attention should be given to the personal cleanliness of the children. They should be taught to wash their mouths daily. Their individual toilet equipment should include the things necessary for this purpose.
>
> The morning toilette should be directly supervised by the teacher responsible for the group and likewise when the children wash their hands before meals. Twice a week *at the very least* they should be bathed or have a shower with hot water, if possible, without omitting the head, as this will prevent parasites. (Sunday morning may be reserved for this purpose.) In the absence of other methods, canals, rivers or other shallow bodies of water may be used by the children to wash their feet and legs every day.[34]

The stress on cleanliness is reinforced in the pamphlet by carefully chosen images: one captioned "Washing her teeth", for example, shows a pretty and spotlessly clean young girl from Cuart de Poblet in Valencia cleaning her teeth in a scene reminiscent of advertising images for products such as Pears Soap.[35]

Reading the IBMA images within this wider archival context enables us to appreciate the depth of their agency and the success of their performance as visual representations of a utopian future. It also brings to the fore their ambiguity and their potential for multiple and conflicting readings. On the one hand, they can be read as part of a progressive discourse of educational reform and improvements in child health and welfare. The images employ the relatively simplistic device, familiar to us from the iconography of the period, of using images of children to symbolise hope and renewal, and to firmly project the colonies as sites for educating the future. The colonies shared a number of elements, such as the emphasis on active citizenship and self-government by the children, also found in the children's "communities", "villages" and "republics" founded by progressive educationalists associated with the New Education movement as a means of dealing with children displaced, or "damaged", after the Second World War, and this is reflected in the images, which are similar in nature, for example, to photographs of the "Children's Republic" at Moulin-Vieux par Lavaldens-Isère in France included in a special issue of *New Era* in 1948, or images associated with the international Pestalozzi village at Trogen.[36]

---

[32] *Children's Colonies*, 13.
[33] For example photographs D/31-33 in the IBMA, Box A/2.
[34] *Children's Colonies*, 10 (emphasis in the original).
[35] Ibid., 11.
[36] *New Era* 29, no. 8 includes a number of articles on children's communities with images of self-government by children; Mary Buchanan, *The Children's Village: The Village of Peace* (London: The Bannisdale Press, 1951).

In addition to promoting an idealistic portrayal of the Spanish Republic's commitment to children, the depiction of the children's participation in labour and collective decision-making also represents the place that children could play in the evolution of a different and new world. A sense of active agency is conferred upon the children, who are represented as individual actors in their own right, contributing to the relief effort on a practical level through growing food and taking responsibility for their own care and that of younger children, and on an ideological level through their participation in the formulation of a new way of collective living. The pride and joy of the boys in Figure 2 is in direct contrast to some of the other images of children from Spain in the IBMA and in other images circulating in humanitarian campaigns, such as that shown in Figure 3, where the subjects are cast firmly in the role of passive victims of the conflict to elicit political support or humanitarian aid.[37] Brothers identified a consistent representation of children and refugees as passive victims in the press photographs which formed the basis of her study, and Kevin Myers has similarly identified the same characteristic in activists' representations of the Spanish children evacuated to Britain during the Civil War.[38]

On the other hand, the images can equally be read as examples of a "controlling gaze" – a reading that situates the colonies as sites of surveillance and discipline, of "social control in the name of enlightenment".[39] The use of photography as part of systems of surveillance and control is well documented, and the colony images existed alongside a recording system that documented the child's physical and educational condition on entering the colony and closely monitored their progress whilst they were there.[40] Rather than seeing the children as active agents, as in the earlier reading, we now see passive subjects who are educated and "civilised" by ever-present teachers constantly supervising the children's behaviour.

Given the important role accorded to the teachers in *Children's Colonies*, there is a surprising lack of adults anywhere to be seen in the photographs. Again, this is open to multiple interpretations: it may serve to remind the viewer of the children's vulnerable and displaced status, separated from their parents and reliant upon the altruistic care of the state. Janet Fink, in her study of child imagery in the literature of the British National Children's Homes, identifies a similar absence of adults, which she suggests was intended to convey to the viewer that despite the promotion of a "family-like" atmosphere, these were not "normal" families.[41] However, the absence of adults can equally be read as a sign of the children's autonomy, self-reliance and agency, indication they are capable of managing their own behaviour. Burke and Grosvenor have argued that a lack of adults is a feature of the iconography of progressive education.[42] Interestingly, British visitors to colonies

---

[37]Fundraising leaflet issued in Birmingham, Library of Birmingham, Acc 2008/51; see also for example IBMA Box A2: File D/51 and 52 which show injured and destitute children.
[38]Brothers, *War and Photography*, 143; Kevin Myers, "The Ambiguities of Aid and Agency. Representing Refugee Children in England 1937–8," *Cultural and Social History* 6, no. 1 (2009): 29–46.
[39]Martin Jay, *Downcast Eyes: The Denigration of Vision in Twentieth-Century French Thought* (Berkeley: University of California Press, 1994), 382–3.
[40]Tagg, *The Burden of Representation*; *Children's Colonies*.
[41]Janet Fink, "Inside a Hall of Mirrors: Residential Care and the Shifting Constructions of Childhood in Mid-Twentieth Century Britain," *Paedagogica Historica* 44, no. 3 (2008): 287–307.
[42]Catherine Burke and Ian Grosvenor, "The Progressive Image in the History of Education: Stories of Two Schools," *Visual Studies* 22, no. 2 (2007): 155–68.

Figure 3. Pamphlet printed and circulated in Birmingham c. 1937 (courtesy of the Library of Birmingham).

also remarked on the children's self-control and consequent lack of supervision which went hand-in-hand with self-government. Helen Grant, for example, on a visit to the colony in Pedralbes, was particularly struck by the fact that none of the children were in any kind of uniform and there seemed to be no obvious supervision in the garden at all – it was taken for granted that the children would behave properly.[43]

However, the trace of one unseen but ever-present adult is unmistakeable – the photographer. Even without corroborating contextual evidence, it is possible to reconstruct a sequence of photographs (to which Figures 1 and 2 belong) as potentially being part of a body of work by a single photographer. The lack of contextual information accompanying the images was remarked upon earlier and as far as it is possible to tell, only one of the colony photographs in this sequence bears the name of a photographer, G. Benete or Benite, working under commission for a government department.[44] The fact that the images do not routinely bear the name of the photographer is not surprising; it was common in Spain in this period for images to

---

[43] Helen Grant Papers, MS ADD 8251/II, 15–16, 19.
[44] IBMA Box A/2, File D/16, stamped on the verso with the words "Ministerio de Estado, Prensa Extranjera, G. Benete [or Benite] Fotografico. Cliche no _____ Fecha_____." Both the plate number and date are blank in the original. The image is further stamped "Spanish Medical Aid Committee, 69 Great Russell Street, London WC1."

remain anonymous, and for the photographers to have no control over the subsequent unattributed use of their images in political campaign materials.[45]

Comparing the IBMA photographs to other images of this period illuminates the photographer's use of visual conventions that would resonate with the audience. The little girl returning the photographer's gaze in Figure 1, for example, evokes Robert Capa's iconic images of children in the Civil War, where a child's eye contact with the camera is often used to create a sense of intimacy between the child, the photographer and the viewer.[46] The images also utilise what Mendelson has referred to as "the iconic status of the peasant", used repeatedly in photographs, documentary film, postcards and posters of the Civil War period to represent the contribution of rural labour to the struggle, to productivity and to stability.[47] The agricultural labour of the young boys in Figure 2 clearly speaks to this tradition and can be seen at work in other sources from the period, such as a pamphlet of political cartoons by Josep Obiols which includes an image of three boys that is almost identical to the photograph in Figure 2.[48] The images also appear to draw on Soviet iconography, both in the use of agricultural symbolism and in the style of photographing children and young people, which is reminiscent of the highly stylised photographs of young male and female pioneers by Aleksandr Rodchenko.[49] Similar images were also taken in children's institutions in the Soviet Union to illustrate the process by which the child was prepared for integration into wider Soviet society, and the themes are much the same – classroom and dining-room etiquette, culture, collectivity, regularity and hygiene.[50]

The other adult presence that hovers over the images is of course the viewer. For the international humanitarian and political campaigners for whom the Spanish Civil War became a major cause, the visual was a key method of communication, providing unequivocal proof of both the reforming and modernising zeal of the Republic and the need for action, and the photographs in the IBMA are part of this tradition. Images were widely distributed and collected and effectively used for propaganda and fundraising purposes by a range of political activists and humanitarian relief organisations. Virginia Woolf, for example, in her discussion of photographs in *Three Guineas*, written in the winter of 1936–7, describes receiving photographs of

---

[45]Mendelson, *Documenting Spain*, 95; Epps, "Seeing the Dead," 133.
[46]See J.P.F. Aizpúrua, R. Wheelan, and C. Coleman, eds., *Heart of Spain: Robert Capa's Photographs of the Spanish Civil War* (New York: Aperture, 1999); C. Capa and R. Wheelan, eds., *Children of War, Children of Peace: Photographs by Robert Capa* (Boston: Bullfinch Press, 1991). The best known example is probably the much reproduced photograph of a young girl lying on sacks taken in Barcelona in January 1939.
[47]Mendelson, *Documenting Spain*, 174–5.
[48]J. Obiols, *Auca Del Noi Català Antifeixista I Humà*. Comissariat de Propaganda de la Generalitat de Catalunya, Sabadell, 1937, LSE, Spanish Civil War Collection, Misc 91 volume 27/3, microfilm 514. Published in Catalan, Spanish, French and English, the English title being *Life of a Catalan, Free as a Catalan's Must Be*. As in the photograph the central figure has his arms around the shoulders of his comrades; the only difference is that in the cartoon, two of them are looking in the opposite direction to that in the photograph and the boy on the right is a fairly stereotypical representation of a black child. The English caption for the cartoon is "His religion is not cheap, it's a hearty comradeship."
[49]Margarita Tupitsyn, *The Soviet Photograph 1924–1937* (New Haven, CT: Yale University Press, 1996), 79–85, 106–12.
[50]Elena R. Iarskaia-Smirnova and Pavel Romanov, "Interpreting Visual Memories of Soviet Institutional Child Care" (paper presented at ESSH Conference, Amsterdam, March 25, 2006).

"dead children" with the words: "The Spanish Government sends them with patient pertinacity about twice a week".[51] Relief agencies such as Save the Children and the Quaker Friends Service Council made widespread use of photographs of children in their fundraising, as the example from Birmingham seen in Figure 3 demonstrates. References in the correspondence files of the British Friends Service Council archives show that images taken in southern Spain were sent to the American Friends Service Committee offices in Philadelphia for wider distribution.[52] The files include numerous references to demand for images from America, Britain and elsewhere, such as the letter from Elise Thomsen at Barcelona to the Friends Service Council in London on 2 July 1937, stating that she and her colleague Alfred Jacob had found a helper to go around taking photographs of colonies, prompted by a regular flow of letters from Paris requesting "descriptions and pictures".[53] Similarly, the Birmingham Quakers – who were quick to respond to the outbreak of war in Spain, forming a Spanish Relief Committee in 1936 which supported two colonies for refugee children at Rubí and Caldas de Maravella in Catalonia – asked the relief worker Francesca Wilson to write a pamphlet on her return to Birmingham, specifically requesting that she should "be on the lookout for new photographs" with which to illustrate it during her stay in Spain.[54]

Given the numbers of British activists visiting Spain, and their keenness to acquire photographic evidence for propaganda purposes, it is not surprising that some of the photographs found their way into archival collections in Britain, the USA and elsewhere. Images comparable to those in the IBMA appear in the papers of individual activists held among the photographic collections of the British Imperial War Museum (hereafter IWM) and in collections of propaganda such as the Spanish Civil War collection in the Archives of the London School of Economics (hereafter LSE). To explore the consumption of the photographs and their journey into British archival collections I want to briefly consider how a moment in one child's experience of learning at Benicasim Colony in 1937 came to be visually represented in three different British collections. The photographic archive of the IWM includes a photograph showing a child sitting at his school lessons at Benicasim. An identical image is to be found in the LSE Archive, this time reproduced as part of a double-page spread on Benicasim in a lavishly illustrated, multi-lingual booklet describing the International Brigades' work with children. The booklet employs photo-montage to juxtapose scenes of learning, smiling children and beautiful homes on the one hand, with images of battlefields, evacuations and children peering apprehensively at the skies above from the entrances of underground shelters on the other. The same child can also be seen in the IBMA, this time in a series of four

---

[51] Virginia Woolf, *A Room of One's Own/Three Guineas* (London: Penguin Classics, 2000), 125, first published by the Hogarth Press in 1938.
[52] For example, Friends Library, FSC/R/SP/5 includes a list of negatives sent to Philadelphia. The Friends Service Council was the arm of the British Quaker establishment that co-ordinated Quaker relief in Spain and had its headquarters in London. It collaborated closely with its sister organisation, the American Friends Service Committee, which co-ordinated American Quaker relief and its headquarters were in Philadelphia.
[53] Friends Library, FSC/R/SP/1/2.
[54] Library of Birmingham, Warwickshire North Monthly Meeting, Spanish Relief Committee, minutes February 25, 1937 and March 11, 1937.

photographs showing classroom scenes captioned "Children's Colony, Benicasim: 1937".[55]

The internal evidence in the images indicates that they form part of a series taken on the same occasion within a short space of time, but what was the route which brought them into three different British collections? The IWM photograph is included in an album of photographs collected by the activist Winifred Bates during her time in Spain.[56] The IBMA is based on papers collected by the International Brigades Association (of whom more later) and subsequently added to from the personal collections of other Brigaders.[57] The photographs under discussion in this study reached the IBMA between 1987 and 1990 and the catalogue states that they include "W. Bates' pictures of refugees in Barcelona". Although a few of the images clearly bear her name on the back, it is not possible to be certain how many in total came from this source, and some undoubtedly came from the collections of other activists – either directly from the individuals involved or their families, or collected together by the historian Jim Fyrth as part of his research for a book on the "Aid Spain" campaigns in Britain.[58] As well as photographs collected by individual activists during their time in Spain, information stamped on the reverse of several of the images indicates that they passed through, or in some cases potentially originated from, agencies such as the Spanish Press Agency, Servicio Español de Información, CSI Service D'Informacion et de Propagande and Spanish Medical Aid Committee in London, a fact which again clearly points to the active collection and circulation of images for use in fundraising and propaganda publications. The duplication of particular images in a number of collections indicates a widespread practice of collection and exchange among individual activists and humanitarian and political organisations.[59]

This use of the visual was part of a wider discourse of aid in which written episodes from children's life stories were used and circulated in a similar fashion. These episodes frequently appear to directly incorporate the child's own voice, although it is impossible to assess the degree of adult translation or mediation involved. The Friends Service Council *Bulletin,* for example, reprinted personalised stories of individual children reproduced from the correspondence or reports of relief workers in Spain as a means of encouraging financial donations to fund its relief activities and to demonstrate the value and effectiveness of the Friends' work. One such instance in the *Bulletin* for 4 January 1937 tells of the "shattered homes" of 10-year-old Anastasio Rodriguez and 12-year-old Carmen Caras, before quoting a third unnamed child described as silent, shy and aged about five:

> He uttered ingenuously the cause of his sadness in four words – "They turned me out." I asked from where. "From school and from home," he answered. The poor little chap

---

[55] *Los Niños Españoles y Las Brigadas Internacionales*,?Barcelona: Comité Pro-Niños Españoles de las Brigadas Internacionales, [?1938], LSE, Spanish Civil War Collection, Misc 91 volume 42/4, microfilm 517. IBMA Box A/2, File D/117.
[56] Imperial War Museum Photographic Archive, HU 33021. Winifred was the wife of the Socialist novelist Ralph Bates and worked as a journalist and for the British Medical Unit, see Jim Fyrth and Sally Alexander, eds., *Women's Voices from the Spanish Civil War* (London: Lawrence and Wishart, 1991), 42, 63–7.
[57] *International Brigade Memorial Archive: Catalogue 1986*, Vol 1.: v.
[58] Fyrth, *The Signal Was Spain*, 1986.
[59] Janina Struk has identified similar repetition of visual images in British and American collections relating to the Holocaust; see Struk, *Photographing the Holocaust*, 13–15.

felt a stranger everywhere, since he had lost his home. Lost homes! How much they mean, how much they account for![60]

Similar episodes appear in International Brigades publications, symbolising the just nature of the cause for which they had travelled to Spain. In *The Story of a Spanish Child*, a child's letter is apparently reproduced in which Antonio Perez provides a brief autobiography, outlining the hardships and tragedies of his young life before his arrival in a colony where, for the first time, he enjoys a happy childhood:

> I am very happy here, enough food and a good bed. I may say that my life has completely changed, we have play things, a library and affection. We take walk [sic] and study.

> I am happy to feel this affection of the International comrades. My heart is also full of love for them who want to make us fit for a better future.[61]

Antonio's letter is reproduced alongside another letter from an International Brigader to his own son at home explaining why he is in Spain, presumably included to ensure that the resonances and parallels between children in Spain and the readers' own families were not lost on the audience.

Such use of a child's life story by activists and reformers, and the apparent incorporation of the child's own voice or testimony, was of course not new – similar techniques had been in use by philanthropic and charitable organisations since at least the early nineteenth century.[62] It was used, for example, by Eglantyne Jebb of the Save the Children Fund in its campaigns to counter child starvation in Europe after the First World War. Jebb articulated the effectiveness of this rhetorical device in an article entitled "Life Stories of Hungarian Children", where she wrote:

> The little autobiographies which have been written by fifty pupils in the Save the Children Fund workrooms in Budapest... explain more clearly than could be explained by any number of dry, statistical, adult written reports, both the need to bring succour to the starving children of the slums and the soundness of the system which has been adopted with this end in view.[63]

I have written elsewhere of the popularity of this device with other women humanitarians who, in their texts, display a similar tension to that seen in the visual sources, between the need to depict the children as passive victims for political or fundraising purposes and the representation of the children as self-reliant and active agents who realise that their future lies in a mutually supportive and communal way of life.[64]

---

[60] Friends Library, London, FSC *Bulletin* no 3, January 4, 1937, 2.
[61] *Los Niños Españoles y Las Brigadas Internacionales*, ?Barcelona: Comité Pro-Niños Españoles de las Brigadas Internacionales, [?1938], LSE, Spanish Civil War Collection, Misc 91 volume 42/4, microfilm 517.
[62] See for example Shurlee Swain, "Sweet Childhood Lost: Idealized Images of Childhood in the British Child Rescue Literature", *Journal of the History of Childhood and Youth* 2, no. 2 (2009): 198–214.
[63] Eglantyne Jebb, "Life Stories of Hungarian Children," *The Record of the Save the Children Fund* 3, no. 1 (1922): 27–32.
[64] Including the author, suffrage activist, and humanitarian aid worker Evelyn Sharp (1869–1955) and the American Quaker journalist and author Anna Louise Strong (1885–1970), both of whom undertook relief work with the Friends in war-torn and famine areas in the 1920s and 1930s. See Siân Roberts, "'I promised them that I would tell England about them': A Woman Teacher Activist's Life in Popular Education," *Paedagogica Historica* 47, nos. 1&2 (2011): 155–72.

MODES AND MEANING: DISPLAYS OF EVIDENCE IN EDUCATION

This article has attempted to articulate the trajectory of the images from their initial creation in Spain as objects to witness and perform the reforming and progressive zeal of the Spanish Republic through their collection, use and exchange as part of the visual economy of humanitarian and political activism to raise awareness and money. I want now to conclude by turning to the later stages in their biography and looking more closely at their incorporation into the particular archive in which I first encountered them, and the subsequent implications of this archival context for their continued performance and meanings.

Archives, as one visual historian of the Holocaust has argued, "are not neutral spaces; they impose their own meanings on photographs" through their processes of selection, ordering and cataloguing.[65] The body of images that prompted this paper was incorporated into a very particular archival context as part of the International Brigade Memorial Archive, which is itself held in the Marx Memorial Library in London.[66] The IBMA was initially assembled and organised by the International Brigade Association, an organisation formed in February 1939 by British volunteers who had fought in Spain and which was closely associated with the British Communist Party. The Association's aims were to continue the campaign against fascism, to support veterans and to preserve and publicise the legacy and memory of the Brigade.[67] The archive was presented to the Marx Memorial Library by the Association in October 1975, a month before the death of Franco.[68] The Association's intention was clearly articulated by Nan Green, then secretary and herself a former activist in Spain, who described the aim as "to build such an archive, which will remain in Marx House as a permanent memorial to the men and women who fought", and this purpose was further reflected in the collection's title: The International Brigade Memorial Archive.[69] Since this initial deposit, the archive has been added to through subsequent gifts of personal collections amassed by individual activists and donated to by the families of International Brigaders.[70] As mentioned previously, the archive also includes material gathered by the historian Jim Fyrth in the process of writing his study of the "Aid Spain" movement in Britain and his subsequent book, with Sally Alexander, on the role played in the conflict by women from English-speaking countries.[71] In this final stage, therefore, with their incorporation into the IBMA archive, the performance and meaning of the images shifts: they are no longer active agents in a humanitarian campaign but rather commemorative objects, incorporated as part of an archive dedicated to addressing the historical

---

[65] Struk, *Photographing the Holocaust*, 13.
[66] The Marx Memorial Library in London is an independent library and registered charity dedicated to the history of Marxism, Socialism and the working class movement; see http://www.marx-memorial-library.org.
[67] Tom Buchanan, *The Impact of the Spanish Civil War on Britain: War, Loss and Memory.* (Eastbourne: Sussex Academic Press, 2007), 138, 177.
[68] Natalie Ann Stuart, *The Memory of The Spanish Civil War and the Families of British International Brigaders,* PhD diss., de Montfort University, 2001: 22–23, 137.
[69] Letter from Nan Green to IBA members, 17 August 1974, IBMA Box A-6, D138, quoted in Stuart, *The Memory of the Spanish Civil War*, 137.
[70] Ibid.; see also *International Brigade Memorial Archive: Catalogue Vol 1 1986*, London, Marx Memorial Library, 1986: v; for more detail on the commemoration of the International Brigade in Britain see Stuart, *The Memory of the Spanish Civil War*.
[71] Fyrth, *The Signal was Spain*; Fyrth and Alexander, *Women's Voices from the Spanish Civil War*.

silence about the British International Brigades and the wider "Aid Spain" movement and providing a "memorial" to their activism.

In her study of images of the Holocaust, Janina Struk commented on the relationship between the past and the present in photographs which have been deposited in a range of commemorative archival institutions. Writing that "[t]he present always has its own agenda for reconstructing the past", she prompted her reader to consider whose story, therefore, is in fact told by the photographs?[72] We could ask the same question of our images – whose story do they tell? Is it that of the children depicted in them, displaced from home and family by a brutal civil war; the political and humanitarian activists for whom they became fundraising and propaganda tools; the members of the British International Brigades for whom they stand as a commemorative memorial; or the historian revisiting the circumstances of their production and performance several decades later? As the images and the entangled stories embedded within them travelled through a range of performative spaces and across international borders, they accumulated a number of multiple and intersecting histories and meanings. In the same way that they represented sites of multiple interpretations in the past, they also embed a number of contesting histories and meanings in the present.

---

[72] Struk, *Photographing the Holocaust*, 15.

The Decorated School: cross-disciplinary research in the history of art as integral to the design of educational environments

Catherine Burke

Faculty of Education, University of Cambridge, UK

>This article reports on the opening up of a new, rich seam of interdisciplinary research that brings together historians of education with historians of art and architecture to examine the meaning and incidence of "The Decorated School". It examines the origins of the idea of art as educator in the nineteenth century and discusses how ideas about the education of taste accompanied the establishment of mass education in industrialised nations during the early part of the twentieth century. Some examples of Decorated Schools in Britain and Europe are discussed with reference to the nature of the international and interdisciplinary interpretation made possible by the research network. Finally, some of the challenges of interdisciplinary research in this area are presented, as well as rich opportunities for further exploration. The article concludes that in order to come closer to a realisation of how pupils might have experienced The Decorated School in the past, we need to incorporate histories of children's play-worlds in our project.

Introduction: frameworks of cross-disciplinary research

>The aim of art is to give us noble and pure delights of admiration through beauty... and the certain, practical, pedagogical result of these pleasures is to make souls purer, higher and more noble, more capable of perceiving the splendour of Good and Truth.[1]

During the first half of the twentieth century in Britain, Europe, Canada and the USA there developed a distinct notion that the common school and mass education offered a means by which the attitudes, tastes and behaviours of the majority of the population could be reached and potentially altered. How far this sentiment was linked by personal travel and correspondence across national borders is a question that scholars have yet to begin to explore, but a start has been made through the UK Arts and Humanities Research Council (AHRC)-funded Research Network, The Decorated School. Two years of funding have resulted in laying some of the groundwork for the further global exploration of this vast and rich field that brings together the interests of educationalists, architects, designers and artists towards a

---

[1] Charles Lévêque, "Esthétique," in *Nouveau dictionnaire de pédagogie*, ed. F. Buisson (Paris: Hachette et Cie, 1911), http://www.inrp.fr/edition-electronique/lodel/dictionnaire-ferdinand-buisson/(accessed August 5, 2013).

democratisation of the arts for all.[2] The project's blog, www.thedecorated-school.blogspot.com, has documented and recorded narrative histories of school-based art as integral elements of the buildings and grounds, and continues to be of interest to scholars and the general public across the world. This was and is a global phenomenon, but we have begun the exploration in the UK and Europe, where the establishment of mass education towards the last quarter of the nineteenth century offered for the first time the opportunity to affect the aesthetic sensibilities of large numbers of the general population who lived lives devoid of art and beauty as defined by the middle classes and bourgeoisie. The 1851 Great Exhibition in London, for the French at least, demonstrated the necessity for France to organise artistic and aesthetic education in order to maintain its quality and leadership in decorative and applied arts. Returning to France after visiting the Great Exhibition, Count Léon de Laborde produced a report promoting the union of art and industry and recommending education of taste for the masses through extensive reproduction of works of art in streets, schools and cottages.[3] In England, the Great Exhibition had the effect of suggesting for the first time that art, as a subject, should be an integral part of a liberal education for the masses, "not merely a polite accompaniment for the leisured classes".[4] For some, this was an urgent task if social unrest and revolution were to be avoided. However, this period also witnessed widespread experimentation with art forms, resulting for many in a sense of insecurity about matters of aesthetics. The years immediately following the First World War and the Russian Revolution were characterised by abstraction in art, challenges to traditional forms of expression and major campaigns and agendas set by young modern artists in Europe.

As art was exploding into new forms and formats, architecture was also being changed by the impact of modernism, while new popular forms of consumption and entertainment – including the cinema – brought into focus concerns around the education of aesthetic sensibilities. Spectacle, as Walter Benjamin saw it, was becoming a signifier of modernity. Advances in science and technology were rapidly changing social expectations and were beginning to offer the majority of the population a far wider choice of manufactured goods than they had ever known. Questions began to be asked regarding how the poorly educated might be equipped to make decisions beyond the economic. The art critic Herbert Read (1893–1968) had strong connections with these movements. He was later to write a seminal text, *Education Through Art* (1943), and throughout his career he was a pivotal figure among networks of artists, writers and architects who were at the time dedicated to discovering and inventing new modes of expression in art that should serve society. Thus art in schools could be imagined as not only a creative project, but one that was political and economic too.[5] Read demonstrated through his writing the necessity of bringing together the disciplines of art, education and architecture and was a precursor to the dynamic that is encouraging cross- and multiple-disciplinarity in research today.

---

[2] The period of funding ran from January 2011 to February 2013. The co-investigator was Dr Jeremy Howard, Art Historian, St Andrews University, UK.
[3] Annie Renonciat, "The 'Art at School' Movement in France: Goals, Ideas, Influence (1880–1939)," in *The Decorated School. Essays on the Visual Culture of Schooling*, eds. C. Burke, J. Howard, and P. Cunningham (London: Black Dog, 2013).
[4] Reginald R. Tomlinson, *Children as Artists* (London: Penguin Books, 1944), 8.
[5] Herbert Read, *Art and Industry: The Principles of Industrial Design* (London: Faber & Faber, 1944).

Referring to twentieth-century British murals and decorative painting in general, Alan Powers describes the period from the end of the First World War to the early post-war decades as "a self contained period in its own right in which the nature of art was further explored and debated, and murals were part of the transition between the ideals of the Victorians and the visual languages of modernism".[6] This period has formed the focus of The Decorated School by means of recording and documenting what has existed and survived in the present, as well as posing the question of how these objects, integral to the building and grounds, were produced and received by inhabitants over years in the "common" or state-funded school.[7]

Researching The Decorated School

In the first UK attempt to assess the scale and address the meaning of the phenomenon, historians of education joined with historians of art and architecture to begin to record and evaluate the intention and impact of the decorated "common" school. The term Decorated School was chosen to include all aspects of decoration, including works of art and sculpture, that were commissioned as intended permanent features of the building and grounds, furnishings, textiles and colour schemes. This is distinct from other non-permanent or fleeting objects such as wall charts, paintings or prints. The features we have been interested in have been placed in or around the building with architectural, social and pedagogical intentions.

Schools throughout the world have long been decorated inside and out, with varying degrees of permanence in their features. The more extensive or elaborate the decoration, the more select or elite the school clientele. In Britain, generally speaking, the higher the degree of decoration, the higher the social status of the pupils. The colleges of Oxford and Cambridge, with their elaborate sculptured edifices and richly decorated halls and libraries, are examples of the epitome of the art of decoration in this sense. However, the decorated school as applied by the (AHRC) Research Network is defined as that form of art, colour or artefact which has been purposely introduced in to the school fabric or grounds in order to inform, educate or otherwise stimulate the imagination of the young. What we might call "the common decorated school" when most evident, during the middle decades of the twentieth century, was perceived by those who invested in it as a counterpoint to the "common" home and the remote art museum or gallery. Such associations raise questions about the history of notions of taste and culture in the context of designing environments for educational experience beyond what is normally understood as the curriculum.

The Decorated School as extended architecture

Understanding the power of architecture to organise movement, affect relationships and suggest styles of teaching and learning, traditional or otherwise, has become an effective focus in recent scholarship and research.[8] Attention to school architecture

---

[6] Alan Powers, "The Mural Problem," in *British Murals and Decorative Painting, 1920–1960: Rediscoveries and New Interpretations*, ed. A. Powers (Bristol: Sansom & Co., 2013).

[7] A database of UK murals, sculpture and other integrated art objects has been compiled by the network and is available from the author of this paper.

[8] See for example Roy Kozlovsky, *The Architectures of Childhood: Children, Modern Architecture and Reconstruction in Postwar England* (London: Ashgate, 2013).

has until now explored aspects of the relationship between material design and human behaviour, whether it be teachers' practices shaped by the environment or their purposeful rearrangement of the environment to meet their pedagogical aims. Prosopography has proven to be a useful tool in opening up the terrain of relationships between individuals committed to a common cause and vision of the renewal of the common school. This interest has in turn revealed the vital role played by exhibitions in bringing educationalists, artists and architects together in working relationships that realised in practical form their collective visions of what education might look like in the future. It has also produced new interdisciplinary histories of the design of education in the twentieth century. Walls, doors, corridors, windows and schoolyards have been regarded as components in the interior marshalling of knowledge and exterior projection of the educational values of the state and community. Consideration of the decoration of schools leads to a return to the material and visual cultures of education and necessarily embraces the emotional, sensory and imaginary in school experience.

Accounting for what existed or still exists is fairly straightforward and the research network is building a comprehensive database of what, where and who made the decorated school in England and Scotland initially. Also largely accessible through the traditional methods of historical research are the beliefs and convictions that accompanied the original commissioning of the works of art.[9] It is possible to research the biographies of individual artists and consider their school work in the wider context of their careers, especially as the various Decorated School activities have awakened embedded knowledge belonging to local communities in which significant examples have been located. However, while the histories of the artists and the art are a necessary part of the story, the challenge of cross-disciplinary research in this case is to incorporate matters of use and misuse (or abuse) over time, particularly regarding changes in notions of taste, culture and art that accompanied arguments for and against the intrinsic value of these objects being part of the school environment.

We have learned from the evidence collected to date that many objects have been lost or destroyed – some fairly recently, such as the Barbara Jones mural "Adam naming the animals" at Yewlands school, Sheffield.[10] Certainly, the notion, expressed in the 1930s by Henry Morris (1889–1962), that art might work its "potent, but unspoken, influence" on those using the building from day to day is long lost and has since the 1970s been supplanted by a different set of beliefs and values regarding the relationship between pupils, school buildings and art. What need to be better understood through further research are the drivers of change affecting dominant ways of understanding or imagining the impact of aesthetics in school environments in relation to changing principles and values regarding the democratisation of art's production and consumption. These, in turn, need to be understood within the wider context of commercialisation and reproduction of art in modern and, latterly, digital forms. This is work for the future, but here we can illuminate some of the possibilities by expanding upon the network's research findings regarding the middle decades of the twentieth century.

---

[9] For a discussion of these, see Catherine Burke, "The Decorated School: Past Potency and Present Patronage," *Forum* 54, no. 3, 2012, 456–71.

[10] For the story of the Barbara Jones Mural, see Catherine Burke, "'Education Through Art': The School Mural as Extended Architecture," in *The Black Box of Schooling: A Cultural History of the Classroom*, ed. S. Braster, I. Grosvenor, and M. del Mar del Pozo Andres (Brussels: Peter Lang, 2011).

The silent teacher and the golden method

It is clear that during the inter-war period, the notion of education through art came to be an established principle and aspiration among advisers and inspectors of schools for the young in England and Wales. Behind this movement were a number of individuals who had themselves been educated outside of the state system within culturally rich families and environments, for whom this was a political as well as an educational mission. Each decade, the Board of Education (England and Wales) published a new edition of the Handbook of Suggestions for Teachers, and in these texts we can discern growing attention to the notion that the building itself and the decoration of classrooms might wield an important and durable influence on pupils, their teachers and any other visitors to schools. The 1927 Handbook talks about "the influence of surroundings" and states that the school "by its silent example should do much to set a standard of living and to awaken and stimulate a love of beauty".[11] The silent workings of the decorated school on those who inhabit its spaces day by day are echoed by Henry Morris in the following pronouncement:

> The design, decoration and equipment of our places of education cannot be regarded as anything less than of first-rate importance – as equally important, indeed, as the teacher. There is no order of precedence – competent teachers and beautiful buildings are of equal importance and equally indispensable ... We shall not bring about any improvement in standards of taste by lectures and preachings; habitation is the golden method. Buildings that are well designed and equipped and beautifully decorated will exercise their potent, but unspoken, influence on those who use them from day to day. This is true education.[12]

Within the 1937 *Handbook of Suggestions for Teachers* we find encouragement to seriously consider colour schemes as part of the educational environment; rejecting the drabness of the past is considered a good thing. At the same time, the exact differentiation of colour hues was developing through the work of Amédée Ozenfant (1886–1966), who taught at the London Architectural Association (AA) for a short while (1936–1937) before moving to New York. The documentary film "Children at School" of the same year included scenes of teachers discussing how they could improve their surroundings by applying copious amounts of colourful paint.[13] There is evidence of a prevailing belief in the effect of colours "on the people who spend many hours of the week in contact with them".[14] This interest in colour as a means of educating the eye returned as an imperative for the designers of new schools in the post-war years, particularly in the pioneering Local Authority of Hertfordshire in England. At the same time there was very little knowledge, or even interest, in the sensory experience of the child; it was merely assumed that they would benefit from the "vitality" and "beauty" of their surroundings. The architect David Medd (1917–2009), who had been taught by Ozenfant while a student at the Architectural Association, spent many decades of his life developing the British School Colour Standards and took a less than scientific approach to research. According to

---

[11] Board of Education, *Handbook of Suggestions for Teachers* (London: HMSO, 1927), 27.
[12] Tony Jeffs, *Henry Morris: Village Colleges, Community Education and the Ideal Order* (Ticknall: Educational Heretics Press, 1999), 58.
[13] *Children at School*. Directed by Basil Wright. United Kingdom: Realist Film Unit, 1937. This film is available in *Land of Promise: The British Documentary Movement, 1930–1950*, DVD collection, by various directors (United Kingdom: British Film Institute, 2008).
[14] Board of Education, *Handbook of Suggestions,* 276.

Figure 1.   Grange School mural by Pat Tew.

Kozlovsky, Medd likened the organisation of colour to that of music, "since both used a limited set of elements that were organized within time and space in accordance with the principles of rhythm and harmony".[15]

One of the Hertfordshire schools visited by the Decorated School Research Network as part of its two years of research was Templewood Primary School, Welwyn Garden City. Completed in 1950, this school was designed by a team of Local Authority architects and was celebrated nationally and by its many visitors from abroad as representing a new type of school that was light, bright and colourful.[16] The artist Pat Tew was invited to contribute murals shortly after the school was opened, and three were produced: two at either side of the entrance to the main hall and one covering a large wall in the dining area. The murals at the entrance stand approximately 8' 6" (3m) high by 7' 6" (2.86m) wide.

The murals were commissioned by John Newsom – Director of Education for Hertfordshire at the time – who was a great advocate of the significance of the visual arts in schools, establishing an "Art for All" programme between 1947 and 1953. Hertfordshire County Council had an enlightened approach to its post-war new school buildings which other Local Authorities thereafter followed. All building budgets included a sum for artwork in the new schools. The subject of the murals – children's tales – was established between the lead architect, Albert W. Cleeve Barr, and Pat Tew; the murals at Templewood are similar in subject matter, though not

---

[15]Roy Kozlovsky, "Colourism at Hertfordshire Schools" (paper presented at the AHRC Decorated School Conference at Templewood School, Welwyn Garden City, Herts, June 23, 2011).

[16]The school is still operating successfully, is very popular and has recently raised funds to have the Pat Tew murals restored. See http://thedecoratedschool.blogspot.co.uk/2011/10/templewood-murals-rededication.html (accessed August 5, 2013).

MODES AND MEANING: DISPLAYS OF EVIDENCE IN EDUCATION

Figure 2. Templewood School mural by Pat Tew.

colour, to a collection installed by the artist at nearby Grange Junior School, built at Letchworth in 1952. Integral to the work are elements of surprise and narrative that reward regular and repeated viewing. One example, remarked upon by a past pupil of the school, is a detail of two horses: one black with a white head; one white with a black head.[17] Such anomalies and fantasies were designed to capture the attention of young viewers and stimulate their own capacities for story making. We have no evidence that the murals were used by teachers in their work with pupils, so Henry Morris' intention that they would work their quiet magic on pupils was allowed to happen unaided as long as the object was visible.[18]

Roy Kozlovsky has pointed out how the base colour of the two murals by the hall entrance at Templewood pick up the exact tone of the colour used throughout

---

[17]Past pupils discuss the impact of the Pat Tew murals on them in a short film available via http://www.youtube.com/watch?v=HPC6WXVNiTE (accessed August 5, 2013).

[18]In fact it was very common for the art to be removed from view, especially when new head teachers wished to stamp their own personality on a school. See Burke 2011; 2012 for examples.

the school building's panels and hall ceiling. In making this connection, Kozlovsky has drawn attention to "one of the most endearing but under theorized characteristics of the Hertfordshire school, one which has been lost to us due to its repeated renovations – its vibrant polychromic colour scheme".[19]

Apart from David Medd's education at the AA, this intense interest in colour can be explained by the pivotal influence of Mary Crowley (later Mary Medd; 1907–2005) at the heart of the Hertfordshire Architects Department. Throughout her life to that point, Mary, influenced by her father, Ralph Henry Crowley (1869–1953), had been convinced of the significance of colour in environments designed to support 'the whole child' – a phrase that her father is credited as having invented. She believed it was possible to "build specific spirit with landscape, brick, wood, metal, glass and textile; with shapes and masses and strips of colour... a place of joy in living".[20]

The external and internal worlds of the child

Templewood was a symbol of modernism in its design and its decoration. The foundations of such symbolism were rooted in earlier decades, beyond the UK borders. The reasons for this are found in the coincidence of two concurrent forces: on the one hand, the school hygiene movement; on the other, the increasing influence of modernism in all of the arts, including furniture design and architecture. The modern and efficient school building was considered to be one where one might expect to find every detail of the materials and grounds attended to, in order to afford – through excellence in design – maximum delight, pleasure and a sense of proportionality in accordance with pure function. The most well-known of these experimental school designs have been well documented as they relate to the increased awareness of the importance of light and air for health and well-being.[21] But the history of the idea that it was vital for children in schools to experience aesthetic pleasure or simply have good things to look at has not been so well explored to date. This was a conviction that held for a period following the Second World War but came to an abrupt end during the 1960s and 1970s when there developed, as a counterpoint, a zealous interest in measuring and evaluating cognitive function. During the early 1970s, the impact of the work of leading sociologists and psychologists had the effect that interest in pupils' worlds shifted focus fundamentally. The external material provision of care and welfare that had been a major focus since the inter-war period through attention to beauty, light and air now appeared to be less important than understanding differences between children's individual internal cognitive development. In material terms, this led to experiments measuring the impact on performance of, for example, windowless school buildings.[22] It may not be a coincidence that it is far easier to measure and account for the effects on children's educational performance of ventilation and hygiene and the effects of removing opportunities for distraction than it is the effects

---

[19]Kozlovsky, "Colourism". Andrew Saint, in his seminal *Towards a Social Architecture: The Role of School Buildings in Post-war England* (New Haven, CT: Yale University Press, 1987), also discusses the colour detail of the early Hertfordshire schools.

[20]Mary Crowley's notebook quoted in Catherine Burke, *A Life in Education and Architecture: Mary Beaumont Medd* (London: Ashgate, 2013), 188.

[21]Documented at the time in Alfred Roth, *The New School*, 2nd ed. (Zurich: Girsberger, 1957).

[22]It is interesting to note that a similar change of emphasis occurred with respect to music education during these years. No longer was it vital to listen to "good" music; more important was listening in general and making music.

on the emotions and senses of surrounding children with examples of fine art and design. This was a moment of high confidence in the application of numerical values in the emerging field of educational sciences.

School as a canvas for the arts

The political significance and dimension of The Decorated School during the middle decades of the twentieth century is not at first apparent, but the research network has begun to reveal important connections with notions of democracy and freedom, as well as with equality, choice and informed consumption: all essential to the survival of capitalist societies. The years immediately before the outbreak of war in Europe appear to be significant in the UK and USA in generating the concept of the school as a canvas for the arts. By this time, the impact of the Fascist regimes in Europe was becoming felt in the UK, as many individual artists, designers, architects and resisters fled in the direction of the USA. Many went first to London; some, including Rudolf Laban and Walter Gropius, stayed initially at Dartington Hall in Devon. Several architects and artists took on commissions while temporarily in England. These *émigré* artists connected with educators and architects through commissioned work and thus the significance of the aesthetic in architecture designed with children in mind was understood on the continent of Europe, in the UK and in the USA, where there was also a school decoration movement.[23] Grosvenor has examined the origins and impact of an exhibition organised in the same period entitled "Design and Education"[24] and cites design enthusiast Frank Pick (1878–1941), who stated that the exhibition should "attempt to show, by a right choice, the materials used for teaching in elementary schools might have a beauty and quality which are the first understanding of design".[25]

While it was generally believed that children of elementary school age were unable to discern what was good, bad, beautiful or ugly in art and design, the impact of Henry Morris's notion of "the golden method" was already beginning to be felt. Pick went on:

> The child in the school is capable in his or her degree of responding to this stimulus; so it is important that the pens, the paper, the books, all the paraphernalia of teaching should be chosen with an eye and a touch for that which is stimulating... Schools will remember that they are educating the future consumer, and maybe setting a standard for industry in the next generation.[26]

During the same year a study undertaken by the education department of the Cleveland Museum of Art, USA, into the nature and growth of artistic sensibilities among children was reported in the *Journal of Educational Research*.[27] This study was

---

[23]See Sylvia Rhor, "Educating America: Murals and Public Education in Chicago, 1905–1941" (PhD diss., University of Pittsburgh, 2004).
[24]Ian Grosvenor, "'The Art of Seeing': Promoting Design Education in 1930s England," *Paedagogica Historica* 41, no. 4–5 (2005): 507–34.
[25]Ibid., 510.
[26]Frank Pick, quoted in *Materialities of Schooling: Design, Technology, Objects, Routines*, ed. Martin Lawn and Ian Grosvenor (Oxford: Symposium Books, 2005), 170–1.
[27]Betty Lark-Horovitz, "On Art Appreciation of Children: I. Preference of Picture Subjects in General," *The Journal of Educational Research* 31, no. 2 (1937): 118–37. This was part of a project of research and experimental education which was carried out at The Cleveland Museum of Art between 1935 and 1940, with the aid of a grant from the General Education Board of New York.

fairly typical of research in the early decades of the twentieth century into children's preferences related to their age and stage of development. Such studies reflect the impact across the developed world of Piaget's principles of categorising stages of children's development. In this case a group of children were shown a number of images and asked to choose which they preferred. Our interest in this study is not so much in the method or results but in the timing of the experiment, during the late 1930s, a period that saw much interest in bringing art into close proximity with children who, unlike those in the study at the Cleveland museum, would be unlikely ever to frequent galleries or art museums.[28] The study confirmed the general belief that aesthetic appreciation did not emerge until adolescence and that children in early childhood were more interested in making art than responding to it. Some at the time even suggested that having children attempt to appreciate or evaluate art might be potentially harmful.[29]

The notion of the relationship between the decorated school and education, so clearly articulated by Henry Morris in the inter-war period, was amplified and extended later by Herbert Read and others. *Education Through Art*, first published in 1943, included a short section considering how the physical structure of the school might become "an agent of aesthetic education" – citing as the best contemporary example Impington Village College near Cambridge, designed in 1937 by Maxwell Fry and Walter Gropius.[30] Impington was not decorated with murals or sculptures but was significant as an example of modernist design. In Scotland, too, during the 1920s and 1930s, there was interest and investment in art in the fabric and grounds of school buildings. The artists Jessie King, Ernest Archibald Taylor, Tom Whalen, John Maxwell, Robert Heriot Westwater and Alexander Inglis, for example, all produced work for new schools. Those of Tom Whalen and John Maxwell are the best known, the former producing "Mother and Child/The Bath", a bronze fountain group, for Bernard Widdows' Prestonfield Primary School (1935) and the latter "Neighbourhood Scenes" for Ebenezer MacRae's Craigmillar Primary School (1935).[31]

Elsewhere in Europe, particularly in Scandinavian countries, the notion that children's environments should reflect something of their interests or stimulate their curiosity was becoming evidenced in the design and decoration of new school buildings. The School-on-the-Sound in Copenhagen, by Kaj Gottlob, is an example. Opened in 1937, the school was designed around an oval atrium that ran the length of the school, around which were arranged four floors with balconies overlooking the space below. On the floor of the atrium Gottlob had installed a large inlaid map of Copenhagen, and the ceiling was decorated with a compass rose. At nearby Katrinedal school, also by Gottlob (1933–1934), mural decorations were placed above outdoor washbasins next to the girls' and boys' toilets. Some years later, at Ungdomsgaarden (1944) in Husum, a large ceiling mural by the modernist artist Richard Mortensen (1910–1993) was completed (in 1947). Here it was possible for the youngest "children to lie in bed

---

[28]Other studies referred to include Bonnie E. Mellinger, *Teachers College Contribution to Education*, vol. 516, *Children's Interest in Pictures* (New York: Bureau of Publications, Teachers College, Columbia University, 1932).
[29]Rhoda Kellogg cited in Martha Taunton, "Aesthetic Responses of Young Children to the Visual Arts: A Review of the Literature," *Journal of Aesthetic Education* 16, no. 3 (1982): 93–109.
[30]Herbert Read, *Education Through Art* (London: Faber & Faber, 1943), 297–8.
[31]I am grateful to Jeremy Howard, University of St. Andrews and Co-Investigator in the Decorated Schools Network, for this information.

and look up at the ceiling". According to Mortensen it was impossible to overestimate the importance of children having things to look at.[32]

Artists' contributions to the enhancement of school buildings through mural decoration and sculpture were not limited to Europe during these years or in the immediate aftermath of the war. There were many examples in the USA, as well as in Canada. In Chicago, for example, Sylvia Rhor has discovered that between 1905 and 1943, over 2000 mural panels (approximately 500 cycles) were executed for city schools. These monumental panels lined corridors, auditoriums and libraries of city schools and included examples from some of Chicago's best-known artists. Rhor has studied histories of murals installed in public schools commissioned by the Works Progress Administration's Federal Art Project (WPA-FAP), one of the New Deal relief programmes for artists during the Depression.[33] In Canada, Kirk Niergarth has uncovered the history of a 1934 mural executed by artist-in-residence Harold Haydon at Pickering College, where the principal, McCulley, had firm ideas about the significance of art as part of the fabric of school buildings consistent with those expressed by Henry Morris. In future society, McCulley wrote, art in all its forms shall no longer be the prized possession of a favoured few, but its enrichment of life shall be the heritage of all.[34] One of the most high-profile and influential elementary schools designed during this period was Crow Island Elementary School in Winnetka, north of Chicago (1940). Here, the whole school was designed as an art piece and highly recognised artists and designers were employed on the whole project. The school was designed by Eliel Saarinen and several family members in collaboration with the architectural firm of Perkins, Wheeler and Will. But, while this was so, the director of activities, Frances Presler, resisted the idea of a school mural "lest it designate too definite form of creation thereby inhibiting instead of encouraging child expression". However, in each of the classroom courtyards, individual terracotta creatures were placed within the brickwork at just the height that children might notice them. They were produced off site by Saarinen's daughter-in-law, the potter Lillian Swann, while Loa Saarinen made textiles for the school at her weaving studio at Cranbrook. Eliel's son, Eero, designed furniture and fittings in collaboration with Larry Perkins and Charles Eames. An outline of the entire school was also depicted in raised brick on one of the external walls.[35]

During the war years, the notion of bringing the arts into close proximity with children became strengthened in some quarters beyond the notion of installing murals and other permanent art fixtures. An example of such was the School Prints series, the initiative of a company set up to enable schools to acquire high-quality lithographic prints at low cost.[36] Such confidence in the power of high quality modernist materials to become a potent educational force was associated with recognition of the importance of public education in rebuilding democratic citizenship in the immediate post-war years.

The war stimulated a widespread school building programme in the English counties, affording progressives the opportunity to wipe away the dark and dismal elemen-

---

[32]Catherine Burke (2013) A Life in Education and Architecture. p.167. See also Peter Olesen (2009) Et loft af Richard Mortensen. Copenhagen. KAB
[33]Rhor, "Educating America."
[34]Kirk Niergarth, "Art, Education, and a New World Society: Joseph McCulley's Pickering College and Canadian Muralism, 1934–1950," *Journal of Canadian Studies/Revue dEtudes Canadiennes* 41, no. 1 (2007): 172–97.
[35]Burke, *Life in Education*, 182–91.
[36]Ruth Artmonsky, *The School Prints: A Romantic Project* (London: Artmonsky Arts, 2010).

tary schools that the majority of the population had hitherto experienced and replace them with something new, bright and modern. Stuart Mason, Chief Education Officer for Leicestershire, believed that the majority of children attending school in the 1950s would finish their education and leave school without ever having seen a modern oil painting in a public art gallery. He therefore thought it vital that commissioned art in the form of paintings, sculptures and murals should grace the interiors and exteriors of Leicestershire's new school buildings. Oil paintings hung on the walls of schools suggested both public gallery and private home and the effect was intended to be civilising; large-scale murals with fantastic imagery, but nevertheless concerned in subject matter with notions of education, childhood and youth, were sited within the entrances of schools. Artists and sculptors were commissioned wherever possible to make school-based art. In the 25 Leicestershire schools that were built after the war, each had a large-scale sculpture, relief or mural. Despite unfavourable economic circumstances in the post-war era of reconstruction, Mason ensured that one third of 1% of the total cost of any new school building was to be designated for commissioned public art. These pieces were often placed in the entrance hall or outside on the forecourt, usually attached to the outside walls.[37] Mason, like his counterpart John Newsom in Hertfordshire, was closely associated with the notion that a key responsibility of teachers was to recognise the artist in every human being that might be released through careful environmental nourishment.

Significant individuals who carried on the tradition during the 1950s and 1960s were certain Directors of Education in the regions of England, the inspectorate (HMI) and particular education advisors. Important figures included John Newsom, Chief Education Officer for Hertfordshire; Robin Tanner, HMI for Leeds and Oxfordshire, who divided his life between his two abiding interests of making art and teaching children; and Alec Clegg, who became Director of Education for the West Riding of Yorkshire and whose vision of education always included the notion of "hyacinths to feed the soul".[38] Tanner and Clegg were closely associated with the Elmhirsts at Dartington Hall, which became a mecca for modernist artists, designers and progressive teachers during the middle decades of the twentieth century. This was partly the result of *émigré* artists finding a refuge there during the years and months just prior to the outbreak of war, but home-grown artists were commissioned too. At the end of the war, following negotiations with the Hertfordshire-based sculptor and artist Henry Moore, a large bronze, "The Family Group", was placed at the entrance of The Barclay School in the new town of Stevenage.

Teachers' courses organised at Dartington, first by Clegg and Christian Schiller and later by Tanner, are part of the story of the Decorated School, since they

---

[37]Some examples were described by John Berger in his essay "Artists and School," *New Statesman*, July 27, 1957, 108–9. Artists commissioned for Leicestershire schools included Ronald Pope, Ben Franklin, William Soukop and Peter Peri. In Hertfordshire, Kenneth Rowntree, Julian Trevelyan and Ceri Richards produced commissioned murals for schools.
[38]The term was often used by Sir Alec Clegg, Chief Education Officer for the West Riding of Yorkshire. From a poem by Moslih Eddin (Muslih-Un-Din) Saadi (Sadi), a Persian poet (1184–1291):

If thou of fortune be bereft and of thine earthly store have lefttwo loaves, sell one, and with the dolebuy hyacinths to feed the soul.

In Tim Brighouse and David Woods, *Inspirations: A Collection of Commentaries and Quotations to Promote School* (London: Network Continuum Education, 2006), 42.

provided opportunities for teachers to come into contact with the highest quality arts and crafts on display and to meet and discuss the work directly with individual artists and designers. These activities underscored the belief that it was essential for schools to at least have the potential to become local museums and galleries, to enable children to be surrounded in their everyday experience of school by the best that human artistic intelligence could produce. This was a social discourse: it relied on a kind of acceptance of social and cultural class divisions in society that would not change in the near future. It was the duty of those who were aware of what constituted art to bring it to the child in school and build the confidence of the teaching profession in understanding the role of creativity in education.

Imagining The Decorated School

The research network has been able to begin to fathom the phenomenon and go some way to exploring the scale and the significance of the Decorated School. However, it has proved more possible to begin to understand the changing contours of how it was imagined by adults that children would appreciate art in schools than to account for such an appreciation by children themselves. Given the strong conviction held by powerful voices in society that art was a potential educator, especially if afforded a permanent place as part of the school building, it is also true to say that at the time of the installation of integral art in school buildings very little knowledge was established as to how children experienced art as part of the school environment, or their general consumption and appreciation of art. Historians of education and childhood interested in exploring the experience of past schooling know very little about children's experience of art in schools during the first half of the twentieth century outside of their art lessons. Such knowledge is important if we are to better understand the context in which the view emerged that taste and aesthetic education might be achievable through the artistic decoration of school buildings and their grounds.

We might turn to observer theory and its history to explore this further, but we find that to be adult-centric. Consideration of the child as spectator and the school as a site where art is produced through the act of looking is practically non-existent in the literature. In the history of education and the history of art education there has been important scholarship about the child as artist and children's own production of art, but there is an absence of literature that seriously considers the child as a spectator and appreciator of art. Picture theory has a lot to say about audience, but the audience member is normally considered as an individual adult standing for a time some distance from a piece of art displayed in a gallery. Rarely is a child even envisaged as one who might make meaning out of looking. There is much of contextual importance that has to date been left unconsidered, in particular the role of the space and time framing encounter/s with art objects. The notion that encounters might happen on a daily basis for several years, during which time the child is inevitably developing and growing, altering perspective and possible modes of appreciation, is completely overlooked in such literature, just as the notion of the school building containing works of art is a neglected site for research.

The Decorated School initiative has recorded the accounts of past pupils who have reflected on their memories of encountering large-scale art objects on a daily basis over years, and their reflections tell us something about the relationship between intention and habitation. At Templewood School in Hertfordshire, where Pat Tew's three large murals have stood since the early 1950s, pupils of different generations recalled their presence and their growing awareness of specific detail as they aged. Reflecting on her experience of attending a decorated school in Bishkek, Kyrgyzstan, Julia Lysogorova illustrates the potential of further research in addressing the pupil experience. Constructed in 1936, this school contained within it several murals. In an extended essay recording and recalling her encounter with the murals on a daily basis over several years, she concludes, "The presence of these murals in my everyday life shaped my experience of the school. They are colourful and occupy large sections of wall; and for that reason, they did not make me think of school as an oppressive environment".[39] In Decorated Schools, art objects are so regularly encountered that they can play tricks with memory: as Julia remarks,

> When I started researching the decoration of my school, I had no memory of these reliefs from my time as a student. Possibly the reliefs' monochromatic colour scheme never captured my child's attention, which was more sensitive to colours. Moreover, the foyer of the school was never a place, which I, as a pupil, could connect with a certain activity. The entrance with its reliefs was a transitory area, where I did not stop, but merely walked past to the floor where my classes took place. The storeys of the school reflected the ages of the children. The ground floor was for primary school children, first and second floor for the secondary school pupils. As I was growing up and studied on all the floors of the building, the decorations also grew up with me. They, together with my general school experiences, created a friendly environment and as a result I could certainly call my school a second home. Now as an adult, what interests me is the significance I gave in my childhood to the murals and what role they played in the school's pedagogical ideals.[40]

Conclusion

The Decorated School research initiative has identified a distinct and significant aspect of the visual and cultural history of schooling that merits further investigation. As with any cross-disciplinary research, the tools of analysis take some time to develop and embed in a new and unfamiliar territory, and therefore the article's scope is somewhat limited to raising awareness and drawing attention to the opportunities of further cross-disciplinary collaboration in the future. The geographical scope of the network was necessarily limited to the nation states that were represented as participant members of the network, which included the UK, USA and Canada.

For historians of education and historians of art and architecture seeking to understand the Decorated School in the past, the problem has been that one context implied to explain the phenomenon is art appreciation, which leads to picture theory, aesthetic experience and the like. This is found to be wanting as it pays little or no attention to the view of the child. The other context implied is educational theory, which fails to address the phenomenon since it is concentrated mainly on the measurable and quantifiable in the school, and in the child as producer more than the child as consumer. For most artists who produced work as integral parts of school buildings, theirs was a labour of love and their earnings, if any, were meagre, especially as compared with the earnings of architects at the time. On the whole, they did not expect their work to become part of the everyday didactic apparatus.

---

[39] Julia Lysogorova, "From Frunze to Oz: Impressions of the Soviet and Post-Soviet Decoration of School 6, Bishkek, Kyrgyzstan," in *The Decorated School*, 73–80.
[40] For the full account, see Ibid.

They are more likely to have identified with children's capacities for play and their need to create fantasy, narrative and stories. Therefore, we might end by arguing that the decorated school in all its forms, past and present, sits securely neither in the world of education nor the world of art appreciation, but in the world of the child, especially their play-world – and the best artists and educators who collaborated to decorate school buildings in the past understood this. Maybe this is precisely what Henry Morris meant by the "golden method".

Puppets on a string in a theatre of display? Interactions of image, text, material, space and motion in *The Family of Man* (ca. 1950s–1960s)

Karin Priem and Geert Thyssen

Languages, Media, Culture & Identity, University of Luxembourg

In the past few decades, increasing attention has been devoted within various disciplines to aspects previously considered trivial, among which are images, material objects and spaces. While the visual, the material and the spatial are receiving ever more consideration and the myriad issues surrounding them are being tackled, their convergence in educational settings across time and space has thus far remained underexplored. A travelling photo exhibition, *The Family of Man*, will serve as a starting point in this paper for addressing some of the complexities inherent in this convergence and thus highlight an essential yet neglected feature of education: its reliance on, and creative use of, multiple "modes" of communication and representation when attempting to produce learning effects. As a particular educational constellation that went on to travel throughout the world and interact with the contexts in which it moved, *The Family of Man* was anything but neutral in design. The paper will show just how carefully it was composed to promote meaning-, power-, and knowledge-making in accordance with its mission. This border-crossing installation thus constituted a spectacle of different interacting views, forms, surfaces, lighting effects, panoramas, movements, captions and other factors that aimed to create order among things and people. Nevertheless, the paper argues, "theatres of display" in education such as this do not imply determination and causality of effects, but rather provide "uncertain conditions" within a spectrum of "actors" and "actants". The paper relates this to the manifold affordances of objects, images, places and so on, to disruptions of meaning in their convergence across time and space and to "emancipation" on the part of learners.

Introduction

A particular exhibition – *The Family of Man* – will serve as the starting point in this paper to highlight an essential yet hitherto underexplored aspect of education, namely its use of multiple modes of communication and representation with the aim of producing learning effects. Indeed, *The Family of Man*, which was devised by Edward Steichen (1879–1973) in 1955 and is still deemed the most successful photographic exhibition of all time,[1] represents a constellation in which textual, visual, material, spatial and other layers of representation are combined and staged

---

[1] The back cover of the exhibition's catalogue – Edward Steichen, *The Family of Man* (New York: The Museum of Modern Art, 1955), still reproduced today – proclaims this.

in a "theatre of display". This specific constellation, moreover, went on to travel around the world and intentionally interacted with the contexts in which it moved, thus increasing its complexity. This paper, then, aims to explore what such a border-crossing hybrid of word, vision, form, movement, space and time – among other things – may have offered in addition to what could be revealed by a mere analysis of the individual elements used for it. While *the visual*,[2] *the material*,[3] *the spatial*[4] and so on are indeed receiving ever more attention in disciplines like the history of education, and while the myriad issues surrounding them are increasingly being addressed, the full complexity of education, and its use of and dependence on such matters as converging textuality, visuality, materiality, spatiality and temporality, have thus far remained underexplored. Historically, exhibitions represent sites of meaning-making that have critically influenced educational systems, policies and practices.[5] Their explicit staging of different representation modes is particularly suited to generating insight into the multi-dimensional nature of education in general. Analysing them may help to develop new methodologies for research on similar "wonders of *mise-en-scène*" that have only just begun to be unearthed, such as educational films.[6]

Starting from photographs "documenting" the exhibition and its chief director, whose "view of the world, of humankind, and of the function of photography"[7] played a central role in its assembly process, the paper will attempt to reconstruct this "theatre of display" and investigate some hitherto neglected dimensions. The questions addressed are, first, to what extent and in what ways did the spatial design of *The Family of Man*, its arrangement of the photos in various temporal–spatial contexts, its creation of depth of vision, flow and the like, provoke an educational experience that transcended the effects produced by the individual elements of the show?[8] In other words, to what degree did the whole, rather than the parts, of this constellation act as an educative force? Second, could the exhibition's textual and

---

[2] See, for example, Michael Emmison and Philip Smith, *Researching the Visual: Images, Objects, Contexts and Interactions in Social and Cultural Inquiry* (London: Sage Publications, 2000).
[3] See, for instance, Martin Lawn and Ian Grosvenor, eds., *Materialities of Schooling. Design, Technology, Objects, Routines* (Oxford: Symposium Books, 2005); Karin Priem, Gudrun M. König and Rita Casale, eds., "Die Materialität der Erziehung: Kulturelle und soziale Aspekte pädagogischer Objekte," special issue, *Zeitschrift für Pädagogik*, no. 58 (August 2012).
[4] See, for example, "'Putting Education in its Place': Space, Place and Materialities in the History of Education," ed. Catherine Burke, Peter Cunningham and Ian Grosvenor, special issue, *History of Education*, no. 6 (2010).
[5] Cf. Martin Lawn, ed., *Modelling the Future: Exhibitions and the Materiality of Education* (Oxford: Symposium Books, 2009); Siân Roberts, "Exhibiting Children at Risk: Child Art, International Exhibitions and Save the Children Fund in Vienna, 1919–1923," *Paedagogica Historica* 45, no. 1–2 (2009): 171–90; David N. Livingstone, *Putting Science in its Place: Geographies of Scientific Knowledge* (Chicago: University of Chicago Press, 2003), 89.
[6] See "Education in Motion: Producing Methodologies for Researching Documentary Film on Education," ed. Paul Warmington, Angelo Van Gorp and Ian Grosvenor, special issue, *Paedagogica Historica* 47, no. 4 (2011).
[7] Eric J. Sandeen, *Picturing an Exhibition: The Family of Man and 1950s America* (Albuquerque: University of New Mexico Press, 1995), 1. For the importance of the biographical element in educational matters, see also Geert Thyssen, "Mapping a Space of Biography: Karl Triebold and the Waldschule of Senne I-Bielefeld (ca. 1923–1939)," *History of Education*, 41, no. 4 (2011), 457–67.
[8] Cf. the assessments of the exhibit's emotional impact in Sandeen, *Picturing an Exhibition*, 3, 4, 9.

visual representations, materialities, spatial configurations and the like be understood as actors in a network of meaning-making, as an assembly that mobilises multi-modal resources on the part of visitors as much as on that of the designers and as a drama or spectacle enabling emancipated spectatorship?[9] Third, to what extent did viewers' envelopment in a tour of montages result in the montages of meaning that the exhibition's designers intended to bring about? Can evidence be found of effective symbolic domination through *The Family of Man*,[10] in that specific cultural views on mankind were effectively represented as universal human experiences? Fourth, in what ways may a multi-dimensional constellation like this exhibition thus have acted as a powerful didactic–political tool and, more particularly, as an instrument of imperialist or national internationalism?[11]

The Family of Man: a particular constellation designed to steer and direct

In order to answer these questions, some information is needed about the development of *The Family of Man* and the make-up of the exhibit in all its dimensions. The show premiered at the New York Museum of Modern Art and was featured there from 24 January until 8 May 1955. It is still considered the most successful photo exhibition of all time.[12] Within a Cold War context in which the fear of atomic destruction and the hope for a peaceful future reigned, it centred on the presumed universal elements of humanity. The Family of Man offered a window to the world – past, present and future – through a customised experience of internationalism, which managed both to attract audiences from different layers of society and to unite everything from avant-garde style to popular advertising. Significantly, after having been shown in New York, the exhibit toured the world as an instrument of American "cultural diplomacy", the intention being to convince people across the globe of the legitimacy of US world leadership. Thus, it purposely interacted with the local contexts in which it was transposed. The exhibition attracted millions of visitors, many of whom were visibly moved by what was often their first acquaintance with such a medium.[13] It received enormous attention in the US as much as elsewhere and provoked both international acclaim and criticism. For this exhibition, the end justified the means, as much in terms of installation as in the choice of photographs, texts (including the captions), material format, lighting, etc. To achieve this, Steichen employed multiple, even contradictory, design forms.

The show displayed some 500 photographs grouped thematically around subjects such as love, marriage, birth, childhood, play, family life, work, religiosity, old age,

---

[9]Cf. Bruno Latour, *Reassembling the Social: An Introduction to Actor-Network Theory* (Oxford: Oxford University Press, 2005); Ingrid de Saint-Georges and Jean-Jacques Weber, eds., *Multilingualism and Multimodality: Current Challenges for Educational Studies* (Rotterdam: Sense Publishers, 2013); Jacques Rancière, *Le Spectateur Emancipé* (Paris: La Fabrique, 2008).

[10]Pierre Bourdieu, *Masculine Domination,* trans. Richard Nice (Cambridge: Polity Press, 2001).

[11]See Serge Guibault, *How New York Stole the Idea of Modern Art: Abstract Expressionism, Freedom and the Cold War* (Chicago: University of Chicago Press, 1983); Sandeen, *Picturing an Exhibition*, 113.

[12]A recently published book pointing to *The Family of Man* as one of the most remarkable historical examples in exhibition history is Ludmilla Jordanova, *The Look of the Past. Visual and Material Evidence in Historical Practice* (Cambridge: Cambridge University Press, 2012) (see pp. 109–50).

[13]Sandeen, *Picturing an Exhibition*.

human interrelations, basic needs, studying and learning, hunger, aggression and war. The photographs were said to have been selected from a collection of about six million images sent to New York by professional and amateur photographers from all over the world.[14] Be that as it may, various historical sources allow one to conclude that the photos represented a distinctly western view of the world. Thus, for instance, about two thirds of the images selected for the exhibition were by American photographers. Many of them had already been published in increasingly popular "glossy" US magazines and they may be seen as a frame of reference for how America saw the world and its role in it.

The installation design of *The Family of Man* was not neutral in terms of meaning- and power-creation and was composed as a function of the show's mission. Not only a whole tradition of display but also an entire team of people were behind the ways in which that mission was served by the exhibit, even if Steichen is commonly represented as its main architect, albeit aided by his primary assistant Wayne Miller. While incomplete, as shall be seen, this view highlights an important dimension of the exhibition: its design by Steichen acting as the puppet master, preparing the theatre, imagining the puppets in it and anticipating some of the strings to which they would be – knowingly and unknowingly – attached. For the concrete make-up of the exhibit, he consulted the designer Herbert Bauer, a former Bauhaus scholar who could make use of his rich experience with the aesthetic practice of European avant-gardes of the 1920s and 1930s and the related design of exhibitions and propaganda. Steichen and Bauer exchanged views about how installations and display modes could most effectively create an experience that drew people in and affected their meaning-making, rather than keeping them at a reflexive distance.[15] In view of this mutual concern, the images for the exhibition, for instance, were not chosen for their individual artistic quality in their original format but for the contribution they could make to the exhibition's overall theme and mission. The pictures had to fit into the general visual assemblage of *The Family of Man* and, above all, had "to contribute pace and drama to the story";[16] "the criterion was to portray a message through the assembled whole".[17]

The design, inspired by commercial spaces such as department stores,[18] may be described as an interacting play of different forms, surfaces, theatrical lighting effects, panoramas, movements and captions. The captions, for instance, remained conspicuously silent with regard to the classification and selection of photographs and inscribed pictures used in the show's universalizing plot and "grand tapestry", which also included "brief quotations from the Bible[,] the Bhagavad Gita and legends of the Sioux nation, [ancient Greek philosophers,] and from Shakespeare and James Joyce and others".[19] An important feature of the show consisted in its independence, as an exhibit, from a traditional museum and a fixed space. Tony

---

[14] Ibid., 41.
[15] See Mary Anne Staniszewski, *The Power of Display: A History of Exhibition Installations at the Museum of Modern Art* (Cambridge and London: MIT Press, 1998), 1–57.
[16] John Szarkowski, "The Family of Man," in *The Museum of Modern Art at Mid-Century: At Home and Abroad* (Series: Studies in Modern Art, no. 4), ed. John Elderfield (New York: The Museum of Modern Art, 1994), 13.
[17] Sandeen, *Picturing an Exhibition*, 53.
[18] Tony Bennett, *The Birth of the Museum: History, Theory, Politics* (London: Routledge, 1995), 101.
[19] Szarkowski, "The Family of Man," 14.

Bennett has argued that mobile museum installations, like the one developed by Steichen and his team, were able to "respond to shorter-term ideological requirements"[20] and created constant resonance in the media by moving around and being opened and closed in continuation. For this purpose, the *Family of Man* exhibit, reproduced in several versions for its travels to all of the continents, was composed as a mobile set of elements that could easily be installed in a similar way at any venue. The exhibit's display sites were often spaces temporarily destined for mass audiences where "official culture" was integrated into "popular culture".[21] This was the case in Moscow, for instance, which was perceived as one of *The Family of Man*'s more important stops.[22]

Exhibition spaces, like the museum sites to which they are historically connected, always carry with them inherent contradictions.[23] Inscribed, as they are, in the tradition of World Fairs that spawned national museums and school systems, they juxtapose and order (e.g. nations and cultures), normatively compare (e.g. views and technologies) and function as instruments of governance and regulation in terms of socially standardised rules of conduct, knowledge production, public instruction and so on.[24] They are also venues of potential open access, participation, discussion, criticism, mixing and so on of people from different layers of society. Related to such contradictory aspects of exhibitions, two key dimensions emerge: a largely human-authorial one that shows clear evidence of hidden and apparent control, and one that escapes this authorial stance and points to unforeseen shifts in meaning-making in which human and non-human agents or "actants" may play a role.[25] In congruence with the spectrum of governance, Bennett connects the "birth of the museum" to a "position of power and knowledge in relation to a microcosmic reconstruction of a totalized order of things and people".[26] This connection also clearly applies to exhibits like *The Family of Man*, even from an authorial perspective: Steichen and his team purposely selected, sorted, arranged and subordinated "material" for the show, thereby homogenising and blurring differences in their presentation (e.g. in terms of class, gender, ethnicity, region and culture). In this assembling process, which would influence audiences' gaze and pace, they more or less made invisible all contradictions, particularities, diversities[27] and mediating interventions.[28]

---

[20] Bennett, *Birth of the Museum*, 80–6.
[21] Ibid., 83.
[22] Sandeen, *Picturing an Exhibition*, 95–155.
[23] Bennett, *Birth of the Museum*, 95–102.
[24] See Martin Lawn, "Sites of the Future: Comparing and Ordering New Educational Actualities," in *Modelling the Future*, 15–29, and other contributions in the book.
[25] Bruno Latour, "On Technical Mediation – Philosophy, Sociology, Genealogy," *Common Knowledge* 3, no. 2 (1994): 33–4.
[26] Bennett, *The Birth of the Museum*, 97.
[27] Roland Barthes, *Mythen des Alltags* (Frankfurt am Main: Suhrkamp, 1964).
[28] Bruno Latour, "From Realpolitik to Dingpolitik, or How to Make Things Public," in *Making Things Public: Atmospheres of Democracy*, ed. B. Latour and P. Weibel (Karlsruhe: ZKM, 2005), 14–41.

Figure 1. Edward Steichen working on the model for *The Family of Man* exhibition, 1955. (Source: *Public Photographic Spaces*, 456).

A "theatre of display": multi-modal interaction among actors with uncertain effects

Going back to the metaphor of the puppet master, purposely staging the theatre and preparing the strings by which the puppets would then be manipulated, it could be argued with Bruno Latour that an assumption of maximum causality between the movements of the puppets and the pulling of their strings does not hold. No form of manipulation necessarily implies determination: according to Latour, sources of action and meaning-making cannot be reduced unilaterally to causal origins. What stimulates actions should be thought of as "uncertain conditions" within an extended spectrum of actors.[29] Importantly, the latter can be both human and non-human. From this perspective, objects (including images) have "scripts" or "affordances" that invite people to take on "roles" in their "story". They are part of culturally and historically shaped "mediation" processes that "translate" both artefacts ("actants") and people ("agents") within plots that allow for multiple "associations", unexpected

---

[29] Bruno Latour, *Eine neue Soziologie für eine neue Gesellschaft: Einfürung in die Akteur-Netzwerk-Theorie* (Frankfurt: Suhrkamp, 2010), 104–11.

"redefinitions", "displacements" or "shifts" of meaning.[30] What Latour writes about artefacts could, of course, also apply to spaces such as those of exhibitions.

Other approaches have been put forward that emphasise the high meaning-making potential and manifold affordances of objects, images, places and so on, as well as "emancipated" activity on the part of learners (readers, viewers etc.), for instance by philosophers or by scholars in social semiotics with a multi-modal perspective.[31] One such scholar, who developed a theory on multimodality in the context of education early on, is Gunther Kress. In reference to didactics, he has argued that the "canon" of any curriculum and the "power of teaching" imply only one side of knowledge transfer.[32] The second, as yet under-appreciated, side of how knowledge is conceptualised, designed and achieved relates to power on the part of the learner. Relevant for the analysis of *The Family of Man* is Kress's contention that "an exhibition presents a 'curriculum' for visitors seen as learners".[33] Exhibitions, from this point of view, may be perceived as learning or knowledge spaces that are individually remarked upon, framed, selected, transformed and interpreted on the visitor's/learner's side.[34] Even coherent messages transmitted by exhibitions are, therefore, inevitably subject to different interests, backgrounds, principles and conceptions on the part of the viewers, which need not be "acceptable to the curator (as shaper of the exhibition-as-curriculum to be assessed)".[35] Kress relates these activities and potential epistemological differences to viewers'/learners' individual use of modes representing agency and authority in meaning-making.[36] Modes, for him, are "socially made and culturally available material-semiotic resources for representation". Multimodality, then, "attends to the distinctive affordances of different modes".[37] In educational contexts such as those of exhibitions, material–semiotic resources for representation used by curators, exhibition designers and the like, such as speech, writing, sound, image, gaze, body posture, gesture, movement, objects and spaces in a certain sequence, order, interrelation, placement or selection, are confronted by those of learners/viewers. Thus is formed a complex knowledge space not defined by a single power of meaning-making but inevitably involving "epistemological commitment" on the part of all of the parties involved.[38] One philosopher who shares the multimodalists' affinity with early semioticians such as Roland Barthes and fashionable anthropologists of science such as Latour is Jacques Rancière, who has highlighted an important

---

[30]Bruno Latour, "On Technical Mediation – Philosophy, Sociology, Genealogy," *Common Knowledge* 3, no. 2 (1994): 29–64.
[31]See, e.g., Rancière, *Spectateur Emancipé*; Ingrid de Saint-Georges, "La multimodalité et ses ressources pour l'enseignement – apprentissage," in *"Vos mains sont intelligentes!": interactions en formation professionnelle initiale* (Series: Cahiers de la section des sciences de l'éducation, no. 117), eds. L. Filliettaz, I. de Saint-Georges and B. Duc (Université de Genève, 2008), 117–58; Jeff Bezemer and Carey Jewitt, "Multimodal Analysis: Key Issues," in *Research Methods in Linguistics*, ed. L. Litosseliti (London: Continuum, 2010), 180–97; Carey Jewitt, "The Changing Pedagogic Landscape of Subject English in UK Classrooms," in *Multimodal Studies*, eds. K.L. O'Halloran and B.A. Smith (New York: Routledge, 2011); Gunther Kress, "Recognizing Learning: A Perspective from a Social Semiotic Theory of Multimodality," in *Multilingualism and Multimodality*, 119–40.
[32]Kress, "Recognizing Learning," 124.
[33]Ibid., 128.
[34]Compare with Rancière, *Spectateur Emancipé*, 19.
[35]Kress, "Recognizing Learning," 131.
[36]Ibid., 129.
[37]Ibid., 132.
[38]Ibid., 134.

factor not to be neglected: namely, the "spectacle" or "drama" itself of teaching, exhibition creation and viewing, play and so on. He acknowledges a distance not only between the creator and the spectator of a certain "drama", but also within the "performance" as something autonomous between the idea of the artist and the perception or understanding of the viewer.[39] The performance, in his opinion,

> is not the transmission of the artist's knowledge or inspiration to the spectator; it is the third thing that is owned by no one, the meaning of which is owned by no one but which subsists between them, excluding any uniform transmission, any identity of cause and effect.[40]

It is the spectator's power or capacity, across irreducible distances, to make her/his own associations and dissociations.[41]

Relating this to *The Family of Man*, it must be stressed that Steichen and his team were very much aware that carefully devised visual, material and spatial configurations could exert a powerful influence on the people who experience them. However, they did not expect this influence to be uncertain or susceptible to symmetrical interrelations between human and non-human conditions. What they intended to produce in visitors was a deeply felt experience that all people – they themselves included – were part of one large family. The exhibition techniques used were meant to create a multi-layered, dynamic space that did not bow to the evident limitations posed, for instance, by fixed walls, but instead produced a theatrical show. This was realised in multiple ways: circular, multi-dimensional and even free-standing installations were devised. Images were shown without frames and attached not to walls but mounted on panels, suspended back-to-back or hung on strings floating in mid-air and evoking transparency. They were enlarged, downsized and cropped to create either a dramatic or an intimate framework of seeing. The people depicted on the photos were also adjusted in size to sharpen the exhibition's message from one section to another, so families were displayed as slightly larger than individuals. Steichen and his team occasionally also created three-dimensional views by brushing pictures against each other at a 90-degree angle. Every device was used to avoid "the aura of high art that enforced respectful distance" and the impression of a "high-gloss sacralisation of the artistic photographic print".[42]

By means of photo assemblies, enabling both depth and flow of vision and a perception of images behind images, the objective was to activate and shape and reshape cultural formulae. Whatever angle visitors viewed the photographs from, they were expected to see a certain picture behind all of the pictures: the family that mankind was imagined to be.

The visitors' flow and circulation was also purposely channelled within the show's *mise-en-scene*. At specific points in the exhibition, this channelling was less or precisely more directive.[43] As the visitors entered, they could not avoid being exposed – as in a prologue – to a caption Carl Sandburg had composed specifically

---

[39] Rancière, *Spectateur Emancipé*, 20.
[40] Jacques Rancière, *The Emancipated Spectator* (London: Verso, 2011), 15. For the original, cited in French, see Rancière, *Spectateur Emancipé*, 21.
[41] Rancière, *Spectateur Emancipé*, 23.
[42] Latour, "On Technical Mediation," 61.
[43] Cf. Sandeen, *Picturing an Exhibition*, 46–8; Kristen Gresch, "The Family of Man. Histoire Critique d'une Exposition Américaine" (PhD diss., École des hautes études en sciences sociales, Paris, 2010), 357–76.

Figure 2. Edward Steichen opened the exhibition's world tour in August 1955 at the Corcoran Gallery in Washington, DC
(Source: Sandeen, *Picturing an Exhibition*, 181).

for *The Family of Man*: only one man, one woman and one child existed in the world, namely "All Men", "All Women" and "All Children".[44] Viewers were then steered to the right, alongside a collage of photographs that formed a transparent barrier, and then onto a platform built around a rotunda made of hospital-like curtains, called "the pregnancy temple". From there, they entered the squared centre of the exhibition, showing family portraits from various cultural backgrounds. In this relatively open space they were allowed to circulate freely around the arranged pictures and approach them to inspect details. Subsequently, they were supposed to enter a space in which they were greeted first by a carousel of images of playing children, accompanied by a John Masefield caption: "Clasp hands and know the thoughts of men in other lands". Juxtaposed with this "ring-around-the-roses"-like

---

[44]Steichen, *Family of Man*, 5.

MODES AND MEANING: DISPLAYS OF EVIDENCE IN EDUCATION

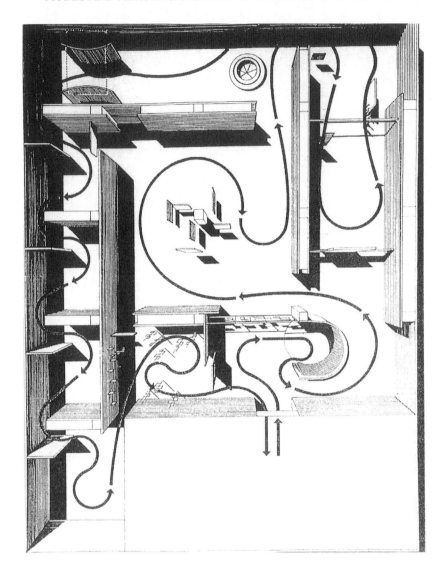

Figure 3. The floor plan for the exhibition in the Museum of Modern Art, 1955 (Source: Sandeen, *Picturing an Exhibition*, 81).

installation, further away two curved panels were mounted with pictures of death and mourning, which narrowed viewers' vision down to a single, oversized image covering the whole opposite wall. Showing New York's Fifth Avenue at midday, it brought life back into the picture, aided in this to no little extent by the caption "Flow, flow, flow, the current of life is ever onward".

Eventually, all the visitors were funnelled between the panels into the narrowest space of the exhibit, but before that, they were given the choice to pass the carousel from the right and enter a dead-end room that displayed pictures of families gathering and celebrating. Once past the curved panels, which can be said to have shown the vices of mankind, the visitors in each case were forced into an enclosing structure that may have been intended to convey angst before giving access to relief.

In this compartmentalised tunnel, Steichen and his co-operators confronted the visitors with displays of aggression, injustice, abandonment and the like – wrongs carefully balanced by harmonising elements that reminded the viewers of the options open to humanity. The trail culminated in an impressively illuminated Kodak transparency of an exploded hydrogen bomb in a black room: the show's only colour print. Its last section was a masterpiece of sentimentalised visions and captions representing hope and redemption by combining an outsized photo of a UN assembly with smaller ones of old couples, a larger picture of a woman's legs richly decorated with flowers, photo stands with children's portraits and, finally, Eugene Smith's "Walk to Paradise Garden" countered by a quintessential image of life: forcefully splashing water. The latter symbolised rebirth through the caption that became one with it: "A world to be born under your footsteps".

In general, the show was successful both in attracting huge audiences and in conveying its message, thereby enforcing a distinctively American view of mankind precisely because of its ingenious didactical use of various modes of representation. *The Family of Man*, in other words, was quite effective in both hiding and conveying its internal contradictions precisely because the different modes, which were intended to communicate its (dubious) message both separately and together, were employed in such a way that all potentially contradictory elements merged to form an homogenising vision. Nevertheless, even at the time it was showing, art critics such as Barthes were refuting the message of the show by pointing out that images always descend from particular historical–cultural contexts, and these particular backgrounds were obfuscated by the exhibition.[45] At the same time it is important to note it was not only art critics who exposed the fallibility of the exhibit's multi-dimensionally composed framing. The general public also responded to the show in ways that "displaced" part of its intended meaning construction. Thus, for instance, a particular picture showing the lynching of a black man in 1930s Mississippi drew a disproportionate amount of attention, disrupting the exhibit's flow and its function as a whole "constellation". Steichen and his collaborators therefore had it removed from the show less than two weeks after its opening.

After its closure at the New York Museum of Modern Art (MoMA), different versions of the exhibition went on tour both nationally and internationally. Edward Steichen and/or the United States Information Agency carefully monitored it – which does not exclude the possibility that audiences responded to its multi-dimensional format in different and, at times, equally unintended ways as they did in the MoMA. To grasp the rich spectrum of these responses, in each case, it is necessary to analyse a broad variety of archival sources, including press clippings and correspondence, which are available at the Steichen Archive of the MoMA and elsewhere. Further, biographical interviews with visitors to the show may have to be conducted, as well as an investigation of what effects resulted from the circulation of the exhibition catalogue – one of the most successful coffee-table books in private households of the time. While, as other scholars have stressed,[46] this catalogue may not do full justice to the exhibit's three-dimensional constellation, it became part of a complex plot of its own, which – depending on its proprietors' or borrowers' means – may also have featured television reports on *The Family of Man*, popular press reviews, commercials shown at movie theatres, and so on.

---

[45] Barthes, *Mythen des Alltags*.
[46] Sandeen, *Picturing an Exhibition*, 175–6.

Be that as it may, it may be stated, as a preliminary thesis, that multi-dimensional plots of an educative nature like these require due attention. Latour-inspired "symmetrical anthropologies", as well as multi-modal approaches from the field of socio-semiotics, could be helpful. They appear to make understandable, for instance, manifold examples of how objects, texts, images and so on are used variably across time and space in "theatres of display" that guide teaching, training and learning processes within well-engineered epistemological frameworks.[47] That is, in classrooms as much as in other educational "sites of display", learning outcomes are not left to chance but are carefully mediated by didactic strategies. These are expected to guide or even dominate learners and what they are intended to learn, know and see. Yet such "symbolic domination"[48] always seems to be susceptible to disruption and displacement in view of the uncertain symmetrical interactions between objects, images, texts, instructors and learners in time and space.

Recapitulating, then, what has passed in review so far, it can be said that interactions between image, text, material and motion were channelled in *The Family of Man* to avoid deviations from the show's intended script. The latter, nevertheless, could be translated according to shifts in meaning created by the ambiguity of human and non-human interactions.

A particular national constellation goes international

As mentioned, *The Family of Man* also toured the world as an instrument of American "cultural diplomacy", intentionally interacting with the local and national contexts in which it was transposed. Thus, it fitted into a propaganda machine that aimed to promote the USA across the world during the Cold War. The United States Information Service (UISIS), a government agency founded in 1953 to improve the political and cultural position of the USA by means of international cultural exchanges, commissioned several copies of the show, including small- and large-sized versions. Both in writings of the time and in recent scholarly work, superlative numbers with regard to visitors, venues and catalogue editions have been used to illustrate the impact of the show's international circulation.[49] While this is a strategy used commonly for various purposes,[50] it actually says little about the show's

---

[47]Latour, *Reassembling the Social*; Latour, "On Technical Mediation"; Latour, "From Realpolitik to Dingpolitik"; Latour, *Eine neue Soziologie für eine neue Gesellschaft*; De Saint-Georges, "La multimodalité et ses ressources pour l'enseignement – apprentissage," 117–58; Bezemer and Jewitt, "Multimodal Analysis: Key issues"; Jewitt, "The Changing Pedagogic Landscape of Subject English in UK classrooms"; Kress, "Recognizing Learning."
[48]Bourdieu, *Masculine Domination*.
[49]Cf. the numbers cited in Szarkowski, "The Family of Man"; Sandeen, *Picturing an Exhibition*; Staniszewski, *The Power of Display*; Lili Corbus Bezner, *Photography and Politics in America: from the New Deal into the Cold War* (Baltimore: John Hopkins University Press, 1999); Jean Back and Viktoria Schmidt-Linsenhoff, *The Family of Man 1955–2001. Humanismus und Postmoderne: Eine Revision von Edward Steichens Fotoausstellung – Humanism and Postmodernism: a Reappraisal of the Photo Exhibition by Edward Steichen* (Marburg: Jonas, 2004); *Public Photographic Spaces: Exhibitions of Propaganda, from Pressa to the Family of Man, 1928–55* (Museu d'Art Contemporani de Barcelona: Barcelona, 2008); Gresch, "The Family of Man."
[50]Theodore M. Porter, *Trust in Numbers: The Pursuit of Objectivity in Science and Public Life* (Princeton: Princeton University Press, 1995); Silvana Patriarca, *Numbers and Nationhood. Writing Statistics in Nineteenth-Century Italy* (Series: Cambridge Studies in Italian History and Culture) (Cambridge: Cambridge University Press, 1996).

impact and moreover makes it seem as if it is easy to verify such numbers through archival research. Indeed, different impressive numbers appeared in publications intended to underline the exhibition's significance and public outreach inside and outside the USA. That said, it is generally stated that after its initial display at the MoMA in 1955, the exhibit toured the world for eight years, making stops on all continents and in three to four dozen countries. This numerical impact of research can be traced back to the exhibition itself, which cleverly incorporated the numerical in its textual and visual representations. Thus, for instance, the "multitude" of pictures distilled from another "multitude" of pictures enhanced the message conveyed by such slogans as "We, two, form a multitude", "We shall be one person", "Before me peaceful, Behind me peaceful, Under me peaceful, Over me peaceful, All around me peaceful...", which shifted attention from the individual to the collective and back, while hinting at infinity.

While circulating, the show had to adapt to local styles of architecture, ornamentation and installation: it was housed in history and art museums, festival halls, palaces of historical value, universities and exhibition halls, and also in department stores and in mobile constructions invented solely for the exhibit. Within historical buildings, the exhibit's installation would incorporate antique-style pillars and ornamental decorations; mobile constructions in turn would consist of modern fibreglass or plastic, as in the case of Moscow in 1959. The exhibition adapted itself flexibly to these varying spatial and architectural circumstances – a malleability mirrored in the show's general ability to meet short-term political requirements. This demonstrates its ability to bring about shifts in meaning-making – over which, however, it had no absolute control. In each case, the changing material shapes of *The Family of Man* added new meanings to it, if only by keeping it up to date and functional as a promising symbol of the future of mankind.

In 1959, though only four years old, the exhibit already found itself operating in a reshaped political atmosphere in which displays of colonialism in all forms were meeting increasing resistance.[51] In addition, the show now featured in settings that returned to the American gaze a reflection on the gaze itself. This implied shifts of meaning that Steichen and his team had not and could not have anticipated. It is in that context that a young Nigerian man, Theophilus Neokonkwo, damaged a number of images from the most popular section of the Moscow *Family of Man* edition.[52] He justified his assault on the photos torn down by pointing to a perceived pattern of display: throughout the show, photographs depicted what he called 'white Americans' and "other Europeans" clothed and thus "in dignified cultural states", while American and West Indian black and Asian people were more often "portrayed either half clothed or naked".[53] Soviet authorities in turn insisted on the removal of a photograph representing a hungry Chinese child asking for food while holding a rice bowl.[54]

Another unforeseen interruption occurred when the show started circulating in Japan. For its opening there in 1956, the image of the hydrogen bomb had been replaced by photos showing victims of the Nagasaki and Hiroshima bombs. This represented an enormous disruption of meaning, in that it shifted attention from a

---

[51] In 1955, for instance, a conference was organised in Bandung at which both representatives of previously colonised countries and newly independent ones met and pleaded for more justly distributed political and economic power.
[52] Sandeen, *Picturing an Exhibition*, 155.
[53] Ibid.
[54] Ibid.

Figure 4. Steichen documented one of the most important moments in the life of his exhibition by contextualizing these representatives of The Other Side into his world family.
Photo: Elliot Erwitt, courtesy Magnum Photos
(Source: Sandeen, *Picturing an Exhibition*, 198).

more general threat of nuclear power to the gruesome effects of America's deployment of this power upon human beings of another nation. In this way, the show's message of universality became untenable. Inevitably, therefore, these new photos were almost immediately removed as a result of UISIS intervention. This is somewhat surprising, considering the special contract that was established between the MoMA and the Japanese publishing company responsible for the organisation of the show.

Meanwhile different copies of the exhibition, with all their material and visual constituents, continued their journey, taking on a life of their own along the way. The UISIS and Steichen himself attempted to control the experiences they induced, for instance by enveloping viewers in the show's picture of mankind, a process facilitated partly by the arrangement of photographs (some of them offering a view onto a life-sized street, inviting them, as it were, to step in and extend the actual exhibition space) and partly by their being photographed in the process, thus becoming included in the show's ever more contested reference frame. A few versions of the show survived until the beginning of the 1960s. In 1964 the American government, through Steichen, donated the last travelling exhibit copy to Luxembourg, where it was opened to the public in the National History and Art Museum (*Musée Nationale d'Histoire et d'Art*). In 1994 the show, after having been deposited in an inadequate storage room, ended up at the castle of Clervaux, where it was later thoroughly restored under the auspices of the *Centre National de l'Audiovisuel* (CNA) (founded in 1989), thus becoming part of the Grand Duchy's national heritage.[55]

---

[55]Back and Schmidt-Linsenhoff, *The Family of Man*; Françoise Poos, "Edward Steichen und *The Family of Man*," in *Lieux de mémoire au Luxembourg II/Erinnerungsorte in Luxemburg II*, eds. S. Kmec and P. Péporté (Luxembourg: Editions Saint-Paul, 2012), 126–30.

Figure 5. The photographs were large enough to envelop their audience, as in Paris, where viewers were inserted into a European street scene. Photo: National Archives (Source: Sandeen, *Picturing an Exhibition*, 185).

The inclusion *of The Family of Man* into Luxembourg's national patrimony had been refused in 1952, when Steichen offered Luxembourg the opportunity to become one of the show's first venues.[56] At that time the country had no more than a meagre photographic tradition, let alone close relations with such museums as the MoMA in New York. Steichen started to receive attention in the country only in the 1960s, when he was discovered by the Luxembourg journalist Rosch Krieps.[57] From then on, his work gradually became integrated into national collections.

---

[56] Poos, "Edward Steichen," 129.
[57] Ibid.

In Luxembourg and other countries, exhibitions later emerged that appear at once to have reinterpreted and revived the traditions in which *The Family of Man* inscribed itself.[58] That *The Family of Man* lost much of its original reference frame but at the same time is preserved, not least in the frame of the UNESCO world heritage programme, gives it a historicity and timelessness for some.[59] Western-orientated programmes such as these,[60] with their stress on restoration and preservation, change the materiality and modality of the show and thus affect its meaning. On the one hand, the exhibit, originally meant to circulate, is now fixed in space – so the installation has lost its flexibility and moved from popular culture to the sphere of art, which could be seen as a move from the public to the archival domain. On the other hand, the exhibit still circulates, but as digital material rather than in physical form. Thus the new technologies, which to some extent increase "emancipated spectatorship",[61] undo any fixation by heritage programmes, Steichen family representatives and others.

Discussion

Among other things, this paper has shown that configurations in which texts, images, material objects and spatial arrangements are staged as a "whole", and the contexts in which this "whole" becomes transposed, matter greatly due to the meanings attached to them and thus the reception of the didactic–pedagogic messages they intend to convey. This paper has also demonstrated that neither the human nor the non-human "actors" in such networks of meaning-making simply let themselves be manipulated as passive puppets on a string. From this perspective, the analysis of photographic exhibitions like *The Family of Man* as specific "theatres of display" is relevant for educational research more generally. It calls upon researchers to take into account all of the actors (both human and non-human) and modes of communication and representation involved in teaching, training and learning, as well as their plural and changing uses. Multi-modal socio-semiotic, Latourian and Rancièrean approaches are thereby viewed merely as possible ways to interpret the complexities inherent in exhibits in particular and education in general. Essential aspects of these complexities appear to be the following: first, an invisibility and

---

[58]For Luxembourg, see, for example, *Images de l'homme dans l'art contemporain/Images of Mankind in Contemporary Art. The 90s: A Family of Man?*, ed. Paul di Felice and Pierre Stiwer (Luxembourg/Dudelange: Casino Luxembourg – Galerie Nei Liicht, 1997). A recent example in the Belgian context, for instance, can be found in the photo exhibition "7 billion Others/7 milliards d'Autres/7 miljard Mensen", http://www.7billionothers.org/ (accessed June 24, 2012).
[59]Sandeen, *Picturing an Exhibition*. Other products of the Cold War, although perhaps less multimodally crafted, also conceal the particular origins and inherent contradictions of their design. Consider, for instance, the OECD and its instruments of "transnational" comparison, such as PISA. Cf. Daniel Tröhler, "The OECD and Cold War Culture: Thinking Historically about PISA," in *PISA, Power, and Policy: The Emergence of Global Educational Governance* (Series: Oxford Studies in Comparative Education), eds. H.-D. Meyer and A. Benavot (Oxford: Symposium, 2013), 141–61.
[60]Cf: Laurajane Smith, *All Heritage is Intangible: Critical Studies and Museums* (Kelpen-Oler: Reinwardt Academy, 2011); Marilena Alivizatou, "Intangible Heritage and the Performance of Identity," in *Performing Heritage: Research, Practice and Innovation in Museum Theatre and Live Interpretation*, eds. A. Jackson and J. Kidd (Manchester: Manchester University Press, 2011), 82–93.
[61]Rancière, *Spectateur Emancipé*.

unawareness of various modes and their different value-loaded uses that make up educational constellations; second, an inevitable hierarchy or inequality in terms of power, if only in terms of "mastery" or available resources to guide learners into a "forest of things and signs";[62] and third, a certain enduring uncertainty in terms of educational processes and outcomes due to the multiple potential associations and dissociations on the part of all of the parties involved (including the spectacle or drama itself of a school lesson, exhibition visit, etc.). These three aspects, and perhaps especially the last one, account for a persistent trait in education – namely the pursuit of control over the uncontrollable through basic forms or formal rules of teaching, training, child-rearing and so on which present well-established and instinctively relied-upon routines. Both the cultural–historical sedimentation and the uncertainty inherent in the convergence of meaning-making modes can be related to the persistence and change – in other words, "order" in "progress" – that Depaepe and others have ascribed to educational processes across time and space.[63]

"Internationalism" adds to the complexities described above and, among other things, situates itself in the communication and representation modes that education uses in different temporal and spatial contexts, since their convergence has particular historical–cultural features. The paper has shown the relevance of travel in the context of a specific multi-dimensional constellation, among other things, by highlighting its crossing of national borders and its blurring of boundaries between the international, the national and the local. Indeed, education constellations like *The Family of Man*, as seemingly ever more "globalised" didactic assemblies, generally appear to be well crafted and offer a fluid economy of meaning and knowledge. Yet at the same time it seems they can become unbalanced by slight disturbances generated in and across local settings. This is related to various and contradictory associations that can occur in webs or networks of meaning-making within and across borders. Be that as it may, it seems necessary for scholars, who are prone to apply "globalisation" theories to school systems, the cultural make-up of schools, classroom practices and even the standardisation of outcomes, to consider such possibilities. In addition, it seems important to point to mutual didactic influences between museums, exhibits, design and architectural projects, commercial enterprises and so on and more obviously educational environments such as schools, as these influences are of vital importance for anyone who wishes to understand the "hard core" of education. In all these – to some extent – educational environments, aspects such as travel and cultural negotiation are involved. This makes the analysis presented here particularly significant for a broader audience dealing with such issues (and debatable concepts) as "internationalisation" or "globalisation", or, one might say, "glocalisation".

---

[62] Ibid., 16–7.
[63] Marc Depaepe et al., *Order in Progress. Everyday Educational Practice in Primary Schools: Belgium, 1880–1970* (Series: Studia Paedagogica, vol. 29) (Leuven: Leuven University Press, 2000).

Index

à Kempis, Thomas 17
Abbt, Thomas 21
Abecedariums 13, 16
act of exposure 42, 60
activism 61–77
actors' multimodal interaction 98–104
adopting German examples 20–32; children's perspectives 23–7; family first 27–9; religion 31–2; role of nature 29–31
aesthetic considerations 68
agency 61–77
AHRC *see* Arts and Humanities Research Council
"Aid Spain" movement 77
Alexander, Sally 76
"Alexis" 29
anonymity 71–2
Archer, Margaret 58
archives 61–77
Areopagitica 56
art appreciation 91–2
Arts and Humanities Research Council 78–80
audience gaze 97–8

Bagnall, K. 43–4
Barr, Albert W. Cleeve 83–4
Barthes, Roland 99–100, 103
Basedow, Johann Bernhard 21–2
Bates, Winifred 74
Bauer, Herbert 96
Bauhaus School 96
Bean, P. 47–8
"before and after" photographs 40–47
Belehem, John 49
Benjamin, Walter 79
Bennett, Tony 96–7
Bhagavad Gita 96
Bible 13, 17, 96
Birmingham Reference Library 39
birth of Enlightened educational poetry 14–20
"Bizarrerie" 23
black communities 49–56
Bondfield Report 1924 37–48

bourgeois ideology 22–3, 27–8
British activists in Spanish Civil War 61–77
British Society 54
Brothers, Caroline 63, 66, 70
brutality 65, 77
Buijs, Jacobus 14–15, 27–8
Buñuel, Luis 67
Burke, Catherine 70–71
Burke, Peter 5
Burmann, Gottlob Wilhelm 11, 13, 20–33

Campe, Joachim Heinrich 21
Canada 36–48
canvas for the arts 86–90
Capa, Robert 72
case studies; children's emigration homes 36–48; dragon's teeth 49–56
Cats, Jacob 14–15, 17
Cavallo, Guglielmo 5
CEHs *see* children's emigration homes
changing technologies 60
Chartier, Roger 5
Children's Colonies 66–70
children's emigration homes 36–48, 56–9; context 36–9; evidence 39–40; texts 40–43; travel/translation 43–8
children's perspectives 23–7
Christianity 19
citizenship 15, 51, 67–8
Clay, Steven 52
Clegg, Alec 89–90
Cold War 95, 104
communication 93–5
Community Relations Councils 50–57, 60
consciousness-raising 51–2
constellation for steering 95–8
consumption 42
context of children's emigration homes 36–9
context of dragon's teeth 49–51
context of encounter 58–9
context of production 56–7
CRCs *see* Community Relations Councils
cross-disciplinary research 78–92
Crowley, Mary 85

INDEX

cultural diplomacy 95–6, 104
cultural practices 2–5

Dartington Hall 86, 89–90
De Imitatione Christi 17
de Laborde, Léon 79
Decorated School 78–92; conclusion 91–2; as extended architecture 80–81; external/internal worlds of children 85–6; in imagination 90–91; introduction 78–80; research into 80; school as canvas for arts 86–90; silent teacher/golden method 82–5
Deken, Aagje 28
democratisation of arts 78–9
Depaepe, Marc 109
"Der junge Baum" 30–31
Der Kinderfreud 22
design of educational establishments 78–92
developing through technologies of display 35–60
"Devoutness" 30
DHA *see* Disability History Association
didactic–pedagogic messages 108–9
directional constellation 95–8
Disability History Association 1
discussing meaning-making 9–10
display technologies 35–60
dissemination of reliable facts 56–60; context of reproduction 56–7; contexts of encounter 58–9; historian's gaze 59–60; image and words 57–8; technologies of production/display 60
Domestic Book for Dutch Families 28
domestic slavery 49
Dr Barnado Homes 40
dragon's teeth 49–56; context 49–51; evidence 51–4; travel/translation 54–6
Dutch poetry for children 11–34
Dutch Society of Sciences 28
Dutch Spectator 28

Eames, Charles 88
Education through Art 79, 87
educational colonies in Spain 61–77
educational establishment design 78–92
educational poetry 14–20
Elias, Norbert 5
emigration to children's emigration home 37–9, 43–8
Émile 12, 21
empire frontiers 35–60
encounter 58–9
Enlightenment 12, 14–20, 25–9, 32–4, 70
evidence of children's emigration homes 39–40
evidence of dragon's teeth 51–4
extended architecture 80–81
external world of children 85–6

Fairbridge Society 38
fairy tales vs. useful stories 14–20
family first 27–9
Family of Man (ca. 1950s–1960s) 93–109
father of Dutch children's literature 12–14
Feith, Rhijnvis 17
Fink, Janet 70
First World War 75, 79–80
fostering 67
Foucault, Michel 59
frameworks of cross-disciplinary research 78–80
Friends Service Council 73–4
Fry, Maxwell 87
Fyrth, Jim 76

Gedichte ohne den Buchstabe R 23
General List of Books for Primary Schools 19, 33
German strategies for moral education 11–34
globalisation 109
golden method 82–7, 91–2
Gottlob, Kaj 87
Grant, Helen 68, 71
Great Exhibition 1851 79
Great Famine 49
Green, Nan 76
Gropius, Walter 86–7
Grosvenor, Ian 70–71, 86
Guernica 66
Guthrie Home 38

Handbook of Suggestions for Teachers 82
Haydon, Harold 88
Heriot Westwater, Robert 87
heritage 8–9
Hiroshima bomb 105–6
historian's gaze 59–60
history of art 78–92
history of migration 3
Hobsbawm, Eric 8
Holocaust 76–7
how meaning is created 1–2
humanitarian aid 61–77

IBM *see* Imperial War Museum
IBMA *see* International Brigade Memorial Archive
image/words 57–8
images interacting 93–109
imagining the Decorated School 90–91
immediate family 27–9
Imperial War Museum 73
imperialism 52, 56–7, 95
improper children's literature 24–5
Inglis, Alexander 87
interaction with uncertain effects 98–104
interactions of image 93–109

INDEX

internal conversation 58
internal world of children 85–6
International Brigade Memorial Archive 9, 62–5, 67–70, 72–6
international constellation 104–8
International Exposition 1937 66
International Standing Conference for the History of Education 1
internationalisation in education 1, 109
ISCHE *see* International Standing Conference for the History of Education

Jebb, Eglantyne 75
Jones, Barbara 81
Journal of Educational Research 86–7
journeying through space 20–32
Joyce, James 96–7
Joyce, Patrick 42
"Joyful Learning" 15–18

King, Jessie 87
Kittsteiner, Friedrich 5
Kleine Lider für kleine Mädchen and Jünglinge 22
Koven, Seth 43
Kozlovsky, Roy 82–5
Kress, Gunther 99
Krieps, Roseh 107
Kuya, Dorothy 51–5

LAA *see* London Architectural Association
Laban, Rudolf 86
Lange, Dorothea 57–8
language didactics 2–3
Las Hurdes 67
late eighteenth-century Dutch poetry 11–34
Latour, Bruno 4–5, 98–100, 104, 108–9
LCRC *see* Liverpool Community Relations Council
Lewis, Green 43
Lieder für Kinder 20–22
Life 66
Little Poems for Children 11, 14
The Little Immigrants 43–4
Liverpool (1970s) 49–56
Liverpool Community Relations Council 51–5, 58–60
Livingstone, David 58–9
Locke, John 11, 13–14
Lodewick, H.J.M.F. 33
London Architectural Association 82
"Love of the Fatherland" 15–16
Lowenthal, David 8
Lysogorova, Julia 91

McNabb, Patrick 49
MacRae, Ebenezer 87
Making of Modern Britain 53

Martinet, J.F. 28
Marx Memorial Library 9, 63, 76
Masefield, John 101–2
Mason, Stuart 89
material interacting 93–109
maximum causality 86–99
Maxwell, Thomas 87
Medd, David 82–5
Mellish, Ilene 53
Melville, J. 47–8
Mendelson, Jordana 72
Middlemore, John T. 37–40, 59
Miller, Wayne 96
Milton, John 56
mimeograph technology 52, 60
mobilising meaning-making 9–10
modernisation 36–7, 72
Moens, Petronella 28
MoMA *see* Museum of Modern Art (New York)
Moore, Henry 89
moral education strategies 11–34
Morgan, Mary S. 43, 56, 58–60
Morris, Henry 81–2, 84, 86–8, 92
Mortensen, Richard 87–8
motion interacting 93–109
moving empire frontiers 35–60; children's emigration homes 36–48; dragon's teeth 49–56; introduction 35–6; reflections 56–60
multimodal interaction 98–104
multimodality 1–10, 99–100; cultural practices 2–5; heritage 8–9; introduction 1–2; mobilising meaning-making 9–10; technology 5–6; translocation 6–8
Museum of Modern Art (New York) 95, 103, 105–7
Myers, Kevin 70

Nagasaki bomb 105–6
National Children's Homes 70
national constellation goes international 104–8
National Council for Evacuated Children 67
national internationalism 95
nature 29–31
Neokonkwo, Theophilus 105
New Deal 88
New Education movement 69
New Era 69–70
Newsom, John 83, 89
Niergarth, Kirk 88

Obiols, Josep 72
Ozenfant, Amédée 82

particular constellation 95–8
Pedagogic Missions 66
Peim, Nick 57
Perez, Antonio 75

INDEX

Perkins, Larry 88
Philanthropy movement 11, 13, 21–2, 32
Phillips, Rodney 52
Piaget, Jean 87
Picasso, Pablo 66
Pick, Frank 86
Picture Post 66
pietism 31
play 16–17, 23–4
pleasure as pedagogical device 14
"The Plum Tree" 33
poetic journey 11–34; conclusion 32–4; fairy tales vs. useful stories 14–20; father of Dutch children's literature 12–14; journeying through space 20–32
Poetry Day (28 November) 33
political stability 36–7
Powers, Alan 80
pre-/post-civil war Spain 61–77
pregnancy temple 101
Presler, Frances 88
producing learning effects 93–5
production 35–60; context of 56–7
prosopography 81
Protestantism 31–2
puppets on a string 93–109
putting family first 27–9

Quakers *see* Religious Society of Friends

Ramey, Jessie B. 42
Rancière, Jacques 7, 99–100, 108–9
Read, Herbert 79, 87
reading for fun 32–4
recognition in Liverpool 49–56
Reformation 17, 32
refugees 61–2
reliable facts 36, 56–60
relief organisations 64, 73
religion 31–2
Religious Society of Friends 61–2, 64, 73
renaissance humanism 56
representation of educational colonies 61–77; humanitarian aid 61–77
research as integral to design 78–92
researching Decorated School 80
respect 49–56
Rhor, Sylvia 88
Rodchenko, Aleksandr 72
role of nature 29–31
Rousseau, Jean-Jacques 11–13, 21–2
Russian Revolution 79

Saarinen, Eliel 88
Saarinen, Loa 88
Salzmann, Christian Gotthilf 21–2
Sandburg, Carl 100–101
Save the Children 64, 73, 75

Schiller, Christine 89–90
school as canvas for arts 86–90
"Schule" 25–6
Schwarz, Bill 36, 56
Second World War 33, 35–6, 40, 69, 85
self-government 68, 71
SHCY *see* Society for the History of Children and Youth
silent teacher 82–5
Smith, Eugene 103
social semiotics 3, 99–100
Society for the Common Good 28, 33
Society for the History of Children and Youth 1
socio-semiotic approach 108–9
Sontag, Susan 43
Soviet iconography 72
Sowing the Dragon's Teeth 58
space interacting 93–109
Spanish Civil War 61–77
Steichen, Edward 93–7, 99–103, 105–8
Stichting Poetry International 33
Story of a Spanish Child 75
strategies for moral education 11–34
Struk, Janina 77
"supremacy of the black" 54
surveillance 63
"The Swallows" 25–6
Swann, Lilian 88
Swildens, Johan Hendrik 16
symbolic domination 104
symmetrical anthropologies 104

Tagg, John 63
Tanner, Robin 89–90
Taylor, Ernest Archibald 87
technologies of display 35–60; production and display 60
technology 5–6
Tew, Pat 83–4, 90–91
text interacting 93–109
texts from children's emigration homes 40–43
theatre of display 93–109; conclusion 108–9; introduction 93–5; national constellation goes international 104–8; particular constellation 95–8; uncertain effects 98–104
Therborn, Göran 50
Three Guineas 72–3
transfer of German strategies 11–34
transformation through technologies 35–60
transforming German examples 20–32
translations from children's emigration homes 43–8
translations from dragon's teeth 54–6
translocation 6–8
transnational history 35–6
travel 35–60; from/to dragon's teeth 54–6; to children's emigration homes 43–8

INDEX

travelling community 7, 9
"Travelling Facts" 58–9; *see also* Morgan, Mary S.

uncertain effects of interaction 98–104
UNESCO world heritage programme 108
United States Information Service 104, 106
useful stories 14–20; *see also* fairy tales vs. useful stories
USIS *see* United States Information Service
utilitarianism 11, 14–20

Vaderlandsch A–B Boek 16
van Alphen, Hieronijmus 11–34
van de Kasteele, Pieter Leonard 31
van den Hull, Willem 18–19

van Eck, Otto 18–19
virtue 21–2, 26
Voluntary Liaison Committees 50
Vom Verdienste 21
vulnerability 42

Weisse, Christian Felix 11, 13, 20–33
Whalen, Tom 87
whether facts travel well 56–60
White Man's World 56
Widdows, Bernard 87
Wilson, Francesca 68
"The Wilted Rose" 29–30
"Winter's Song" 30
Wolff, Betje 28
Woolf, Virginia 72–3